"If just the thought of homeschooling makes you feel like quitting everything, this book will encourage you! In *Homeschooling*, Ginny has a way of meeting you right where you are, with wisdom, grace, and humor. She will help you identify and remove self-imposed pressure so you can see that learning happens best in the freedom of everyday moments. This book will be a breath of fresh air to you, reminding you to lean in, breathe deep, and trust that you don't have to do it all perfectly—you just have to show up and walk in what God has called you and your family to."

**Levi and Jennie Lusko**, bestselling authors of *The Marriage Devotional*

"In an age of hyperchoice and anxiety around all the things our kids could or should be doing, this book is an enormous breath of fresh air. I finished it feeling equipped and empowered while simultaneously feeling relief. Presence, relationship, curiosity, and character matter the most in our education journey. Ginny shows that brilliantly."

**Jefferson Bethke**, *New York Times* bestselling author of *Fighting Shadows*

"If you've ever questioned your ability to homeschool your children successfully, help is on the way! In Ginny Yurich's signature style of informative encouragement, she offers readers the reassurance they need to go the distance with confidence and joy. *Homeschooling: You're Doing It Right Just by Doing It* is a must-read for every homeschooling parent!"

**Heidi St. John**, author of *Becoming MomStrong* and host of *The Heidi St. John Podcast*

"Ginny is one of the most gifted communicators I know. Her newest book is wonderful, personal, practical, and a total pleasure to read. I trust her integrity and wisdom. I loved this book, and I know you will too."

**Sally Clarkson**, speaker, podcaster, and bestselling author

"Ginny Yurich possesses a remarkable ability to inspire a love of learning and adventure in children, a passion she has maintained throughout her life. When the death rattle signaled the likely extinction of innocence and wonder of childhood in America, Ginny kept the porch light on, welcoming families to embrace exploration. In an era where many parents seek alternatives to public education, there is no better voice of encouragement than Ginny's. She has empowered hundreds of thousands of children to reclaim their childhood, reminding us all that childhood and a true education are worth fighting for."

**Alexandra Clark**, host of *Culture Apothecary*
*with Alex Clark*

"One of my favorite things about being an author is when friends write great books and I get to endorse them. This is one of those moments. Ginny is undefeated! Is there anything she does that I don't love? I have the 1000 Hours Outside app on my phone. I have her podcast in my headphones. Now I have this book on my shelf. You should too if there's a part of you that wonders, *What if?* when you think about homeschooling."

**Jon Acuff**, *New York Times* bestselling author of
*All It Takes Is a Goal*

"An instant classic! *Homeschooling* is the number-one essential book every home educator needs today and for generations to come. With her trademark optimism and buoyant spirit, Ginny Yurich is the perfect voice to belt out a new homeschooling anthem that will refresh, refocus, and renew us all."

**Erin Loechner**, bestselling author of *The Opt-Out Family*

"This book will affirm and uplift you if you are already homeschooling, and it will give you the quiet confidence to begin down this path if you are considering it. Deep care for children and parents warmly permeates every page."

**Kim John Payne**, MEd, author of *Simplicity Parenting*,
*The Soul of Discipline*, and *Emotionally*
*Resilient Tweens and Teens*

"Homeschooling parents, this book is your pep talk in print. Covering everything from creating a personalized learning experience to fostering deep family bonds, Ginny Yurich breaks down the myths, builds you up, and makes you feel empowered to lead your kids on this incredible journey. Grab this book and let it remind you: You've got this and your kids are thriving because of it."

**Emily Morrow**, author, speaker, and creator
of Really Very Crunchy

"What an absolute pleasure to be able to celebrate a brilliant friend and a powerful book all at the same time. Some books are informative and some are humorous and lighthearted; this book is all of the above and then some! We have not only witnessed the beauty of homeschooling in our own family for the last seventeen years, but we have

also had the privilege of seeing the Yurich family live out these principles in both the good and the bad, and what a joy it has been. Through
Ginny's engaging and informative way, you will feel seen in your questioning, encouraged in your doubting, and, above all, empowered to
jump into or continue the adventure that is homeschooling."

**Dustin and Sarah Lolli,** lead singer of Sanctus Real and
husband and wife duo, This Way Home

"If you are uncertain about homeschooling, start with this book.
Ginny Yurich proves that she is well-read and thoughtful as she cuts
a path from the experts who influenced her to a place where they can
influence you. This book shows the power wielded by the homeschooling parent for the good of the child. It is a must-read."

**Roger A. Smith,** MD, author of *Parenting with Influence*,
podcast host of *Parenting Matters Now*

"Through reading her new book, *Homeschooling: You're Doing It
Right Just by Doing It,* I understand more fully why Ginny has become
a crucial voice and thought leader in the areas of homeschooling and
nature-based play. I would have given my eyeteeth as a young homeschool mom to have had this book as a companion and resource. It
answers the questions that kept me awake at night: *Am I doing this
right? Am I doing enough? Am I ruining my child?* By reading this book
now, you will save yourself hours of angst in the future. Your confidence
level as a homeschooling parent will soar. Do you have a naysayer in
your life or a family member who constantly questions your decision
to homeschool? Give them a copy of this book, now! If you've been
searching for inspiration and information on taking the leap into the
world of homeschooling, look no further. Ginny Yurich has provided
you with what you need to step into the world of educational freedom."

**Zan Tyler,** speaker, author, podcaster, and founder of the
South Carolina Association of Independent Home Schools

"I wrestled with the schooling system long before understanding why.
It was the writing of amazing educators who came before me that
opened my eyes and put words to what I was inherently coming to
understand. They gave me the strength to build something better for
my family and for others. Ginny's book is reminiscent of those early
days of understanding, and I am positive that it will be a light for so
many who are teetering on doing home education but afraid of what
it looks like. I highly recommend you give it a read and allow it to help
you discard the fear of doing what is best for you and your family."

**Matt Beaudreau,** president and founder
of Apogee Strong Programs

"Ginny Yurich is giving families so many fantastic gifts with her writing and podcasting. She is an essential ally to parents in the trenches of the war to serve our kids well. In her new book on homeschooling, she lays out the foundation of a learning home that welcomes children as children and serves them as human beings. Every chapter informs and inspires, but the chapter on boredom had me cheering! Leaving space for boredom isn't just positive, it's essential for creativity and imagination. And those gifts—so often overlooked by modern educational systems—lead to human beings who flourish in community and culture. Ginny is showing us the way and doing it in her uniquely wise, joyful, and inspiring way."

**S. D. Smith**, author of The Green Ember series

"Those who walk with the wise become wise, and Ginny Yurich stands out as one of the most insightful guides on the homeschooling journey. In her transformative book, she explores ten fundamental principles that you're likely already practicing, illustrating how they empower your child to thrive as the unique individual they are. With a rich blend of her touching anecdotes as a mother and educator, alongside compelling stories and research from others, Ginny weaves a vibrant tapestry of inspiration, knowledge, and empowerment. This book is not just a guide—it's an invitation to nurture the best in your child and in yourself, offering deeper clarity and conviction behind the why of homeschooling so you can approach this journey with confidence and purpose."

**Rachel Kovac**, homeschooling mother of six and writer at Stitched Together

"When my wife and I stepped into 'the great unknown' of homeschooling back in 2014, I wish that we'd had an encouragement like Ginny's! While most people were saying, 'I could never homeschool my kids!' it felt equally scary and exciting to us. The idea of having freedom to teach our kids to love learning in fresh ways, not just kill time in class for eight hours a day so they can remember facts only long enough to pass a test, encourages connection as a family and prepares them for the real world's ever-changing horizon. Ginny infuses her writing with hope and practical wisdom that awaken the senses to all the possibilities at hand when we just say yes to this amazing opportunity to shape our children's lives spiritually, practically, intellectually, physically, emotionally, and even imaginatively. This resource is invaluable if you're even considering turning 'the great unknown' into 'the great adventure.'"

**Stephen Miller**, pastor, author, musician, and speaker

# HOMESCHOOLING

## You're Doing It Right
## Just by Doing It

# Ginny Yurich, MEd

**BakerBooks**

a division of Baker Publishing Group
Grand Rapids, Michigan

© 2025 by Virginia Yurich

Published by Baker Books
a division of Baker Publishing Group
Grand Rapids, Michigan
BakerBooks.com

Printed in the United States of America

Library of Congress Cataloging-in-Publication Data
Names: Yurich, Ginny, author.
Title: Homeschooling : you're doing it right just by doing it / Ginny Yurich.
Description: Grand Rapids, Michigan : Baker Books, a division of Baker Publishing
    Group, [2025] | Includes bibliographical references.
Identifiers: LCCN 2024043379 | ISBN 9781540903419 (cloth) | ISBN 9781493450367
    (ebook)
Subjects: LCSH: Home schooling—United States. | Experiential learning—United
    States.
Classification: LCC LC40 .Y87 2025 | DDC 371.04/20973—dc23/eng/20241230
LC record available at https://lccn.loc.gov/2024043379

Design / Cover illustration: Daniel Neuman

The author is represented by Alive Literary Agency, AliveLiterary.com.

Baker Publishing Group publications use paper produced from sustainable forestry practices and postconsumer waste whenever possible.

25   26   27   28   29   30   31      7   6   5   4   3   2   1

To Nellie, with deep gratitude for more
than a decade of shared joys, challenges,
homeschool holiday parties, and friendship.
*You amaze me. There is so much yet to come.*

# CONTENTS

# FOREWORD

Our culture is in a crisis of inadequacy. The ever-expanding Internet of Things, social media, and techno-sophisticated tapestry make us feel like even humanness is inadequate. How do we keep up with technology, with frenetic, frantic, hurried, harried lifestyles dominated by demands for more?

More beauty requirements. More credentials. More markers of success like bigger houses, snazzier cars, and exotic vacations. Homeschool parents, rather than feeling affirmed and adequate in their decisions, often suffer increasingly from "not good enough" syndrome, which morphs into inadequacy.

When my wife, Teresa, and I decided to homeschool when our firstborn was six weeks old, in 1981, homeschool conventions did not exist. In fact, government truant officers would steal your child and put them in foster care with allegations of negligent parenting. Our decision met with violent disapproval from grandparents and parents steeped in institutional education.

I still shudder at the expectations foisted upon us by these well-meaning relatives who, as Daniel hit six years old, demanded, "Read to me." In desperation, I purchased Mc-Guffey Readers (Hadn't that worked for Laura Ingalls?) and began taking them with me on our farm projects. Suddenly, happy father-son times of working together on the farm became nightmares of inadequacy.

"What does *C* say?"

"K-uh."

"What does *A* say?"

"A-a-a."

"What does *T* say?"

"T-uh."

"Now put it together."

He just couldn't. He began hating books, hating the work of reading, and I hated that I couldn't make it happen. I'd been an early reader as a child, loved reading, loved writing. But here was a son who just couldn't get it. At six. Then seven. Then eight. Not good.

Then Teresa and I received a conservation award and had to leave for three days to travel to Washington, DC, and accept it. We left our two children at the farm with Grandma (my dad had already passed away). Daniel was in charge of the farm—at eight. He moved the herd of one hundred cows by himself each day, handling the water trough, electric fence, and mineral box. But he couldn't read. He could run the farm, but that didn't impress the powers that be. Yet he could memorize long passages of literature when we read them aloud.

At ten, he joined the local 4-H club and was elected historian. I'll never forget the ride home after that meeting.

Piping up from the darkness of the back seat, he blurted, "Well, I guess if I'm going to be an officer, I'd better learn how to read."

In literally a month, on his own, he was reading at a high school level.

Our daughter, meanwhile, was like me. Early reader, took to it like a duck to water, and still loves to read. Two kids as different as night and day, with different interests, different talents, different personalities. But today both are extremely successful, mentors, and high achievers. They are far more than adequate.

Like Ginny Yurich, we took early cues from John Holt and Raymond and Dorothy Moore, and after that initial McGuffey Reader debacle, we went to an "integrate, don't sweat it" protocol. We fully embraced the notion that kids are naturally curious, and if we don't do things to stifle or thwart their innate curiosity, they'll turn out just fine. When Daniel was elected president of the Virginia 4-H at eighteen and shepherded nearly twenty other peers in his elected cabinet, many chided him for not planning to go to college. He created his own answer: "I don't have to sit in a classroom to learn what I need to know."

Because Teresa and I embraced homeschooling before it was a movement, we depended on our kids to satisfy their own learning. In fact, we even believed we weren't responsible for their knowledge; they were. Our responsibility was to incorporate them into our lives; live a life full of purpose, enthusiasm, and discovery; and immerse them in it. We never hired a babysitter.

Many times, at supposedly adult functions, ours were the only children there. They learned to engage with adults, became sociable (saying "yes, ma'am," "please," and "thank you") as opposed to socialized (acting like normal kids), and developed deep relationships with surrogate grandmas and grandpas. Before they were teenagers, our adult friends were astonished at their poise and authenticity and coveted time with them.

Our daughter, Rachel, began a baking business at about six years old. A couple of her girlfriends at church, when they were about ten, launched a little magazine. When Thanksgiving came around, Rachel's contribution to the "what are you thankful for" theme was titled "I'm Thankful for Work." She wrote that if it weren't for work, the world be a chaotic, ugly place. I've never been so proud.

More is caught than taught. If you live your life in front of your kids like you want them to live their lives, they'll learn what they need to learn, both in character and in academics. But that takes time. It takes a platform of affirmation. It takes safety and security, fewer distractions, less celebrity culture, and more butterflies and earthworms.

In this fabulous little book, homeschooling-in-love-with-nature guru Ginny Yurich comes alongside homeschool parents who suffer from inadequacy syndrome. *Do I have the time? Am I smart enough? Am I organized enough?* She's completely sympathetic to the whispers of doubt that cloud our confidence.

Ginny is absolutely correct that the very decision to homeschool and the action to carry it out are bathed in forgiveness. You don't have to be a perfect teacher, perfect parent, perfect organizer, or perfect anything. Homeschooling is wrapped in forgiveness for slippage, imperfections, and inadequacies. As long as we don't stifle curiosity and our children's compulsion toward discovery, they'll be just fine, thank you very much.

This is Ginny's message, and it's as fun to read as it is to implement. A fantastic writer and storyteller, Ginny will reenergize the depressed, lift the downhearted, and inspire the seeker. What a delightful read. Thank you, Ginny, for always putting into words the message we need to hear.

**Joel Salatin**, farmer, author, food freedom advocate

# INTRODUCTION

If our children are to thrive in a world that is rapidly evolving and full of uncertainty, they need less structure and more play.

Dr. Madeline Levine[1]

We always knew.

It often goes this way when you are a public school teacher. When you stand up front and take a view from near the whiteboard or chalkboard, things look different. You begin to see the absurdity of bells. You begin to feel the pull of every unofficial boss—each parent, each administrator, the department chair, and counselors. You begin to realize that decisions are not and cannot be made for the sake of the individual child but only for the group as a whole. There just isn't enough time.

This isn't and never will be an indictment on the teachers themselves, who are (mostly) lovely and who (mostly) put in a grueling amount of work just to stay afloat. These are simply observations on a linear, systematic approach to children, to human beings, who are anything but linear and systematic.

I had a unique situation in my second year of teaching, in which I started at a new school and didn't have a classroom. In those days the school was overcrowded, and as the newbie I was placed in an interior room, which wasn't much bigger than a storage closet, with three other teachers. We called it our cloffice (a new word coined that combined "closet" with "office"), but it actually contained little more than a desk and storage cabinet for each of us. It also included a microwave that was designated for an entire wing of teachers. Many days I came home carrying my bags and a faint smell of microwaved soup or burnt popcorn.

I would emerge each day from our cloffice with a cute cart. It was two-tiered and made with colorful plastic. It wasn't a squeaky metal cart. This cart was fancy, with an ergonomic handle and even a locked storage compartment at the bottom.

My cart held everything. Pens, pencils, calculators, protractors, paper, assignments to return and new assignments to give, scissors, textbooks. It was my life, balanced precariously on top of a fancy cart. And during passing time I would push my cart from one room to the next, moving through the hallways just like the students (who didn't have carts but backpacks).

Standing tall at 5'2", I blended in with the hallway crowd pretty well as a twenty-two-year-old teacher. It was only my cart that gave me away, so when students weren't paying close attention (they rarely were), they didn't use the same language filter they would use in a classroom setting with adults around. Consequence: I heard unbelievably vulgar things on the daily. Occasionally a student would catch my eye in horror, exclaiming, "I didn't mean that" or "That's not what you think it means, Mrs. Yurich." I have said, on repeat, that if a parent would just stand plastered against a high school or middle school wall during passing time for a week or so (possibly even a day), they would seriously reconsider ever sending their child back.

Yet I never saw a parent come to observe. Truth be told, there were hardly any adults in the hallways at all. For a small blip of time, teachers were required to stand in their doorways during passing time to help curb fights. That didn't last very long, presumably because passing minutes are like gold. It's seven minutes of allotted time to reset for a new group of students . . . and to pee.

But even this practice of doorway standing didn't give those teachers my perspective. I was boots on the ground. An infiltrator. Not by choice but by default. And so I didn't get just a day or a week or even a month of passing-time conversation uploaded into my brain; I got years of it. And while it was not every child who said the things that would make even adults blush, every child heard it. I know because I was there.

These days, students often say that the passing times are silent due to rectangular supercomputers glued to their hands. The drama and vulgarity have moved online while still being an ever-present part of each student's day, whether they are participating or not. I'm told by current students, former students, and adults who have visited high schools since the widespread adoption of smartphones that the hallways and lunchrooms are eerily quiet. But this has not solved the problem of vast exposure to X-rated content for teens.

## Times Are A-changin'

In many ways, things are worse for teens than ever before in regard to mental health and well-being, but it was during my firsthand experiences back in the early 2000s, the BlackBerry era, when we knew definitively that this was not the path we were going to take for our kids. Both middle school and high school were out of the question, and our decision for elementary school came on the heels of the widespread adoption of full-day kindergarten across the country.

A bus that came at 8:00 in the morning and didn't return until 4:45 in the afternoon seemed like a grueling day for a five-year-old. So we knew from the very beginning that we were going to be a homeschooling family.

In many ways, we had an advantage of knowing early and definitively that there were no other suitable options for our family. At times every homeschool parent wavers. They waver in their resolve and their confidence, but my experience of the alternative option helped us keep our course.

Our decision came with some seeds for how I envisioned our homeschool looking. These weren't fully fleshed-out ideas, but nonetheless, I had a lot of thoughts floating around about how homeschooling would go before our first child was even born.

Through my training and education, I knew right where to find all the Grade Level Content Expectations (GLCEs— pronounced "glicks," which was reason enough to leave the school system, so I would not have to hear or say that ever again). These were easy to find through the state department of education, and in my mind I pictured a large scroll that I would dramatically unfurl and tape to the wall. I would have the glicks (sorry) printed on the scroll with checkboxes next to each one. Homeschool was to be a checking of the boxes.

> *Kindergarten reading:* "Identify the front cover, back cover, and title page of a book."[2]
> We could even start this before kindergarten. CHECK!

> *Kindergarten reading:* "Isolate and pronounce the initial, medial vowel, and final sounds (phonemes) in three-phoneme (consonant-vowel-consonant, or CVC) words. (This does not include CVCs ending with /l/, /r/, or /x/.)"[3]
> I wasn't quite sure what any of this meant, but I had five years to figure it out. CHECK!

> *Kindergarten history:* "Distinguish among yesterday, today, tomorrow."[4]
> CHECK.

> *Kindergarten physical education:* "Throws underhand with opposite foot forward."[5]
> CHECK.

> *Kindergarten physical education:* "Performs locomotor skills in response to teacher-led creative dance."[6]
> Bonus: I am the teacher! CHECK!

Easy peasy.

Problems arose when the vision of our homeschool, which I had held closely since before my kids were born, intersected with our life circumstances as kindergarten closed in.

For starters, my husband, Josh, and I did not have just one child at that time; we now had four, the youngest having just been born that spring. To recap, that was a five-year-old, a three-year-old, a two-year-old, and a newborn. Additionally, Josh was out of work for a period of time, so getting my scroll printed was moved down a ways on the budget. Finally, unrelated to the job loss, we also found ourselves scrambling for housing because the woman we had been paying our rent to for several years apparently hadn't been paying her mortgage. A foreclosure notice on our front door was the third thing in a trifecta of circumstances that caused me to rethink everything, including my checklist approach to home education.

My mom has always told me to let my smile be my umbrella, so with shaky knees and a wide grin, I began to read a bit more about alternative methods of education. For example, I had heard small strings of conversation about how the Waldorf schools didn't start formal reading training until around the second grade, or when the adult teeth began to come in. It had something to do with body proportions and organs (such as the eyes) being fully formed. And when they did start in on reading instruction, it was with whimsical stories such as the one below. These were whiffs in my mind—like the whiffs of smells you may get walking the loops at a campground. Nothing was concrete, but there were lots of little threads.

The King (emphasize that "K" sound) was in dire need of help. His kingdom (repeat, emphasize "K" sound) had grown large in the land, and every assistant he had asked could not help him peacefully rule this kingdom ("K"). He went to the jester, who would only juggle and laugh. He went to the butler, but he was too busy in the castle. He cried out to the prince and princess, but they were busy with media interviews. The lords had taken off on horseback. Just when the King ("K") was about to give up hope, he heard a small noise. It sounded like "meow." And there, underneath his royal chair, was his royal cat (emphasize "K" sound).

I have no idea if this is remotely close to the story that is actually told in the Waldorf schools, but I do know that phonemic awareness is taught via story, and what a marvelous way indeed to teach language to children.

I had now taken my first step away from "Isolate and pronounce the initial, medial vowel, and final sounds (phonemes) in three-phoneme (consonant-vowel-consonant, or CVC) words. (This does not include CVCs ending with /l/, /r/, or /x/.)"

My midwife, Beth Barbeau, who helped deliver our three youngest children, was sending her sons to the local Waldorf school for a portion of elementary school, and she was the one who exposed me in small measure to Waldorf concepts of rhythm, natural toys, and a different approach to reading. I had also heard that Finland took a different approach to reading, which mirrored the Waldorf schools with an older age of introduction at the very least.

There were two books that caught my attention as well, solely based on the titles. Raymond Moore and Dorothy Moore wrote *Better Late Than Early: A New Approach to Your Child's Education*, and John Holt wrote *Learning All the Time: How Small Children Begin to Read, Write, Count, and Investigate the World, Without Being Taught*.

Without being taught?!

But certainly, I had already seen this firsthand. At that point, we were two years into our 1000 Hours Outside lifestyle, a tagline I coined and a movement I started in 2013 with the goal of getting outside for 1000 hours in a 365-day period. It was in nature, and within the myriad of hands-on, embodied experiences we were having indoors as well, that I realized I didn't have to explicitly teach how to distinguish between yesterday, today, and tomorrow. My young kids would automatically dance whenever I turned up the music and danced with them. And they could throw underhand in many types of circumstances—lying down, feet together, one foot forward.

For many families, the early-childhood years they've spent in nature doing the 1000 Hours Outside challenge has given them the confidence they need to make alternative educational choices for their kids. When we combine large swaths of self-directed time, open spaces in nature, and age-appropriate freedom, kids grow. They don't grow in the checkbox sort of way. But they grow in their own way. Their own beautiful way. The pressure subsides. We don't have to control so much.

Our child's first five years of growth happened without a checklist. And yet, he grew.

As I began to peruse the lengthy list of glicks (last time, I promise), I began to question, "Why am I starting this checklist approach now?"

In Michigan, kindergarteners are expected to count to one hundred by ones and tens. Is there a long-term impact if this doesn't happen until the first grade? Or even the third grade?

I came to the shaky conclusion that maybe the assigned tasks with timelines weren't as important as I initially thought they were. Maybe they were more for the sake of classroom management, order, and moving children through a systematic K–12 experience from teacher to teacher and building to building.

Could we stray?

I had no choice but to dip my toe in the water and try something else.

My insides screamed against this. I wanted control. I wanted a checkbox on a scroll that would signify to my brain and my nervous body that I was doing this "right." That I wasn't messing up our kid.

## Stepping Into the Unknown

When we were firmly planted in this space of no-man's-land, where I had only slight glimpses of other research and felt like I was forging ahead with my eyes closed, I started to meet other homeschoolers.

K–12 public education is rather methodical. You can imagine my surprise when others began to ask, "What kind of homeschooler are you?"

Huh?

"What are the options?" was my initial reply.

"Well, you could be classical, Charlotte Mason, un-schooler, eclectic . . ." The list went on.

"Is there an option for the parent who has no idea what they are doing?"

I am the I-literally-have-no-idea-what-I'm-doing kind of homeschooler.

But the initial question ushered in more confirmation that there are many paths to becoming educated.

Still, I was on edge for two and a half years. Other kids were starting to read. Our son was still illiterate.

We had a new family from church over for dinner one evening. Both of our oldest sons were in the first grade. Their son went to traditional school and could read. Ours couldn't.

"What do you do for homeschool?" the mother sweetly asked.

"Nothing," I replied.

I've since learned that is the wrong answer. Not only because she was shocked (and their family never came over for dinner again), but also because we actually were doing everything. It just looked different.

In our home, all the subjects were woven through our play experiences, read-alouds, and hands-on living.

Age seven came with a rush of relief. Our son's adult teeth were coming in, which signaled something about body proportions and fully functioning eyes (I was still a little shaky on all the details). We embarked on a book called *Teach Your Child to Read in 100 Easy Lessons*.[7]

To me, the title is the antithesis to everything you hear about reading in the United States. I'm not sure where the sentiment comes from, but learning to read is often touted as grueling. In fact, in Michigan a new requirement was passed after I left the teaching field, stating that all teachers, regardless of subject area expertise, are required to take two courses in the teaching of reading, "one of which must be completed prior to earning an initial standard teaching certificate, and the other of which must be completed prior to advancing to a professional teaching certificate."[8]

In other words, you cannot have a professional teaching certificate (no matter what subject you are teaching) unless you have taken not only one but two courses on the teaching of reading. Whoa, this must be hard.

There are instances where the teaching of reading does require extra skill and expertise. A child who is dyslexic, for example, may need varying levels of support at different ages and stages of the process. And certainly, if two separate trainings are required for every Michigan teacher in the teaching of reading, there was no way I, as a parent without training, would be able to pick up a book for less than $20 and teach my own child using "easy" lessons.

I tried it anyway. There were no other options.

So we began. And it turned out that we didn't even have to finish the entire book.

Each lesson took ten to fifteen minutes. Our son went from being completely illiterate to reading chapter books by lesson 74, at which point we put the book back on the shelf. It took less than twenty hours of "easy" instruction, which we did together, seated shoulder to shoulder.

I do not advocate and will never advocate a one-size-fits-all approach to education. This book may not work for your family. But it worked for ours. That $20 investment went a long way. It cost us exactly $5 per child for them to learn how to read (and if you're confused about the math because you know that we now have five kids, there will be more on this later). There were no tears. There was no struggle.

I write this with a heart sensitive to friends who have had struggles with the teaching of reading (or other subjects). The point of the story, the point of the deviation from the scroll, is *not* that any of this comes with a guarantee of ease. The point is that there are ways outside of traditional methods that may work for your family and your kids. We can veer off the well-worn path of glicks (I lied, but I am truly done now) and time frames and straight-line education.

This is undoubtedly scarier. I don't have any checkboxes to prop me up. I don't have any checkboxes that I can use to proclaim to the world, "I'm doing it right." But what I do have are thriving children in a world where a vast and increasing number of children are struggling.

You may be coming to home education from any number of situations.

Maybe, like I was at one time, you have yet to give birth, but something in you already knows that this is the path you will take.

Maybe you are in the preschool years, and the question is looming. Others are starting to ask. You are feeling the pressure. You know deep down that you want to keep your children with you. You know they will thrive at home. But you are scared—scared of doing it "wrong" and messing them up.

Maybe you are in the process of adopting, and you know that home is the place of rhythm and respite. You have no qualms about the level of care and love you will provide at home, and yet you're not completely comfortable carrying the full weight of educational responsibility.

Maybe your children have already begun their educational journey, and your original choice is just not working for them. They are not being challenged enough, or they're being challenged too much. There could be a bullying situation that's occurring online, in person, or both. Possibly your child is just being asked to sit for too long, for too many days in a row. Maybe there are behavior issues—ones that dissipate during summer vacation—that you know stem not from naughty behavior but from a mismatch between biology and expectations. Kids are meant to move in order to learn. They come into the world as boisterous balls of energy, and the classroom environment often is not conducive to the way that children innately are.

Maybe you want something better, more vibrant, for your teen or tween than eerily silent hallways and lunchrooms.

And so you embark—or you make the intention to embark—with the biggest question looming: "Am I doing this right?"

It's the question that all of us face. The wording may vary slightly.

Am I doing this right?

Am I doing enough?

Am I messing up my child?

But the root concern of the question is the same.

What I emphatically believe, based off a decade-plus of research as well as hundreds of conversations with subject-matter experts on our podcast, *The 1000 Hours Outside Podcast*, is that the simple choice of keeping your child home means you are doing so many things right before you even put pen to paper.

I will walk you through ten main things you are "doing right" just by keeping your kids at home, but know that there are many more. This list is by no means exhaustive.

For the parent who is making that initial choice, nervous and with shaky knees like every parent, this list will give you the confidence to say yes, knowing that you don't even need to know what "type" of homeschool family you are in order to get a lot of things right from the very beginning.

For the parent who is weary, this book will be your go-to pick-me-up, a place of refuge that reminds you of your why. We all need encouragement at times, and you will find it here.

For the parent who is living through either overt or subtle pressure, expectations, or questions from extended family and friends regarding your educational choices for your family, this book serves as a manual that can be given or referenced if things get dicey. Whether you win others over to your view or not, your answers to their doubtful inquiries will be found in the pages ahead.

For the parent who needs to prop up a friend, you can hand them this book. You can talk about the topics discussed within to strengthen your resolve.

We need each other. Our kids need each other. Your commitment to the homeschool community as a whole will leave a generational impact.

My educational world started with a single cart, two shelves, and one locked area underneath. I began in a cloffice.

Today, education oozes out not only from our entire home but also into all the areas we frequent in our surrounding community and beyond. Amazingly, our teens can distinguish between yesterday, today, and tomorrow even though I never checked the box. Even though I'm not sure if they learned that in kindergarten or when they were four or when they were eight.

Choosing to home educate has been the best choice we have ever made, by far. Kids thrive at home, and surprisingly, even though it doesn't make much logical sense, parents do too.

Get ready to give yourself a high five or pat yourself on the back. Here are ten things you're already doing right, simply by choosing to homeschool.

# You Are Learning
# Through Living

Living is learning and when kids are living fully and energetically and happily they are learning a lot, even if we don't always know what it is.

—John Holt, *A Life Worth Living*[1]

In the third grade we were each given a small, round plastic container that we set on our desks, filled with something that seemed like bedding, and added mealworms. The goal was to have the mealworms turn into beetles right there on our desks. I don't remember the beetles, only the mealworms, so I'm not sure if it worked or not. Maybe other students ended up with beetles while my mealworms perished? Either way, it was exciting to watch something live and wriggling around in a container on your desk—albeit for only a few weeks.

As I scroll back through the catalog in my brain, I can think of very few experiences that happened during my K–12 education where I learned through actually doing something real. Experiential learning tends to be the exception rather than the norm in the traditional school model. This isn't to say that the teachers didn't try. When I was a high school mathematics teacher for five years, I tried as well. The students sat in teams of four and we played games, but still we sat in a walled-off room with no windows, disconnected from the outside world.

It is hard not to replicate that approach when you transition to homeschooling because you aren't aware of anything else. And if you don't approach learning in a systematic, checkbox sort of way, there are a lot of gaps between what a child knows and what we know they know. And that feels uncomfortable. We want to have a clear picture of what they understand so we can write it down, attach some data points to it, and move on to the next thing. It's like stacking blocks—setting one piece of knowledge on top of another, as high as we can go. If our child learns something and we don't know they learned it, how will we stack the next block? As John Holt's quote above emphasizes, we must embrace the fact that children learn immensely from simply living— experiences that are rich in lessons yet often elude quantification. It's a trade-off. But it's a good trade-off.

## Personal Journey: From Classroom to Homeschool

I attempted the systematic approach for a while. There are a lot of programs available that will walk you step-by-step from kindergarten through twelfth grade in a scaffolding-type way. If this works for your kids and your family, stick with it. There is no one right way to homeschool. No matter which curriculum approach you take, whether it's fairly exact or more open or even no curriculum at all, your family will continue to live life outside of schooling. There will be open minutes and hours, sometimes weeks or even months, when you will experience life in seemingly inconsequential moments and major milestones, like welcoming a new baby into the family.

It is often those moments of blank space during the day that make our knees wobble. Where is the checkbox for "spends an afternoon building LEGOs"? Or "makes a mess of the kitchen"? Or "transfers water from one container to another over and over again"? Or "reads the same books for the nineteenth time"? And because there is no checkbox for these types of open-ended, child-directed activities, their worth is suppressed. It's not stated, but it's felt. We fret and bite our fingernails, feeling like we are failing and flailing, because in the school system, every minute is accounted for. It seems as though the teachers and the kids are making the most of their time, while we are frittering ours away on random things.

Yet John Holt said, "We learn to do something by doing it. There is no other way."[2] My K–12 educational experience didn't include much "doing it," except for the mealworms. There was occasionally a facade of doing something, but most often, school was listening and taking notes, textbooks and exams.

To get a better grasp on this, I took a step back to consider what new things I'd learned as an adult. Interestingly, it wasn't all that much. I had put education and growth in a box for my own self. I completed my K–12 education, went on to get a few degrees, and then closed that chapter, entering into a professional career that required some tweaks and adjustments but no major growth. I was doing what I had always

31

been fairly good at. Honestly, it felt good. I felt competent. I cannot remember a time I failed. And if I had never stepped away from that career, if we had gone the traditional route of daycare and K–12 education for our own children, I would still be making minor tweaks. I would be twenty years in. New kids, same job. And maybe I would've gotten enough seniority by now to have a classroom with windows, but my day in and day out would be an endless flow of pluses and minuses, epsilons and deltas.

Instead, here I sit writing the book that is in your hands. It is technically my eighth, though five of the eight were self-published. Eight books! I can hardly spell. That is not a joke. I am constantly asking my husband (and now my older kids), "How do you spell 'occasion'? Are there two *s*'s and one *c*? Or vice versa? What about 'Tennessee'? 'Penitentiary'?" That last one is really hard. It may seem like a random word, but it's often been said that on average, kids today spend less time outside than people in jail do—so I needed to know how to spell "penitentiary."

Not only am I not a great speller, but I'm also not highly creative. Math brains are black and white. They usually aren't (at least mine isn't) artsy or flowy. They aren't great at interior design, style, photography . . . or writing. I spent the majority of my college years not writing full paragraphs. I wrote sequential lists of symbols to hopefully end up at equal signs.

The question is not whether one life experience is better than another. The first scenario with the twenty-year veteran teacher serves up much less stress. It is known. It is unflappable. It comes with incremental pay increases and a retirement package that can be counted on. It comes with security.

I walked away from all that out of necessity. Out of a calling to the next generation that we were raising. And I did lose all the things I listed above. I lost a foundational sense of security, which isn't insignificant. What I didn't know at the time was how much I would grow as a person. How? My growth came through doing.

We can look at our very own lives, reflect on where we've left the comfort of known skills for whatever reason, and see how we grew by doing. We grew by experiencing. We grew by trying. We grew by failing.

## Challenges of Traditional Education

I broke from my original intentions when we went with the Finland/Waldorf approach of delaying formal education by just a few years. Still, I was drawn to that systematic style of learning. It helped me feel better, more competent. And yet, I would continue to read books about homeschooling that challenged my thinking.

Spending at least a little time furthering your own learning about educational philosophy goes a long way, especially when your brain contains thirteen years of only one path. There are many schools of thought out there about what an education is and how to get one. I read those books with some trepidation. It is challenging to read about other options, other ideas. It forces new considerations and critical thinking. It prompts change.

After reading certain passages about education, I would often think, *I wish I hadn't just read that*, because I couldn't move forward in the same way. I would have to jump ship and try something else. That was my responsibility as the parent. As I learned more, I expected more of myself for the sake of our kids.

One paragraph that stopped me in my tracks is from "The Seven Lesson Schoolteacher"[3] by John Taylor Gatto, which appears in his book *Dumbing Us Down: The Hidden Curriculum of Compulsory Schooling*. The passage comes from an acceptance speech that Gatto gave when he was named New York State Teacher of the Year in 1991. I don't throw this book title around at the Thanksgiving table, but it sure is a strong one—especially coming from a Teacher of the Year in the state of New York. Some of the chapter titles in *Dumbing Us Down* are just as chilling as the book's. Chapter 2 is titled "The Psychopathic School," and chapter 4 is "We Need Less School, Not More." These words flow from the mouth of a man who was in school for three decades—thousands upon thousands of days.

"The Seven Lesson Schoolteacher" is a series of seven unspoken lessons that kids learn at school, which are taught implicitly by the very way the system is set up. There are lessons like confusion, indifference, and provisional self-esteem. No teacher sets out to be confusing. In fact, quite the opposite. And yet, because all this learning for thirteen years straight is out of context and doesn't come from living, classroom learning is fragmented.

Gatto boldly states, "School sequences are crazy. There is no particular reason for any of them, nothing that bears close scrutiny. Few teachers would dare to teach the tools whereby dogmas of a school or a teacher could be criticized, since everything must be accepted. School subjects are learned, if they can be learned, like children learn the catechism or memorize the Thirty-nine Articles of Anglicanism." The result? "I teach students how to accept confusion as their destiny."[4]

Contrast that with sequences that come naturally. Gatto lists "learning to walk and learning to talk; the progression of light from sunrise to sunset; the ancient procedures of a farmer, a smithy, or a shoemaker; or the preparation of a Thanksgiving feast."[5] These are all quite different from the disjointed, subject-specific, age-specific approach we take to K–12 education.

I hope I've whetted your appetite to read the remainder of "The Seven Lesson Schoolteacher." It's witty and thought-provoking. It will give you something to fall back on during the days when you doubt yourself.

While most of the lessons simply give me resolve or a better understanding of the value of home education, lesson five on intellectual dependency gave me a kick in the rear to make a change. Gatto explains how we spend basically our entire childhood dependent on someone else to tell us what to do with our learning. And there is no behind-the-scenes peeking as to why or how this is all determined. From that first day of school, you implicitly learn that your job is to try to construct the systems of knowledge that your teacher tells you to construct—even though, up until that point, you've learned a tremendous amount all on your own.

Neurotypical children learn to walk without one bit of formal instruction, often before they've even spoken a word. They can't complete a worksheet or comprehend a lecture about walking, and yet something on the inside of them guides them through one of the most complex skills known to the human race. Getting robots to walk is a challenge. In a fun book written for kids, titled *Building Robots with*

*LEGO Mindstorms*, the authors write, "Animals and human beings use a very complex geometry operated by an impressive number of independent muscles."[6]

The same can be said of talking (Have you ever tried to learn a new language as an adult?) and of so much more that happens in those early years of life. There is no intellectual dependency during this stage.

Then a child turns five. We buy them a special back-to-school outfit and a new backpack that we fill with pencils, crayons, and a lunchbox. Anticipation and excitement are high. We take photos of the special occasion. It all seems so normal. Everyone else appears to be doing it. But what are we actually sending our kids to? We are sending them to a place that completely undermines their own instincts to learn. They were already learning independently. They were learning quite a bit, actually. Complex things.

Gatto writes, "Good students wait for a teacher to tell them what to do. This is the most important lesson of all: we must wait for other people, better trained than ourselves, to make the meanings of our lives."[7]

I was convicted. I was doing this in my home. It was well-intentioned. But every bit of planning for our homeschool stemmed from me. I was deciding everything.

When I took a step back, I realized how living out a childhood in this way had hampered me when I finally left behind the public education model. As long as I stayed on this narrow path, one foot in front of the other, I knew what to do. But when I stepped away from it, when the world opened up, I felt both lost and unsure of myself. A large swath of my childhood had been given over to others to determine how my time would be spent, both in and out of school.

This phenomenon has only worsened over the past decades as homework loads have both increased and stretched their tentacles into lower and lower grades. It is not uncommon to hear of early-elementary school students having homework assignments these days. At the very least, when I was growing up, my afternoons, weekends, and summers were free for many years into my schooling.

As our children's days are becoming increasingly structured, we're also seeing major shifts in the job market. In 2016 the World Economic Forum wrote a report called "The Future of Jobs," where they stated, "65% of children entering primary school today will ultimately end up working in completely new job types that don't yet exist."[8]

In 2016 Alison Kay, a global business executive with more than twenty-five years of experience leading and transforming businesses, wrote about research done by Richard Foster, who lectures at the Yale School of Management. Foster's research "revealed that the average lifespan of a Standards & Poor company has shrunk from 67 years in the 1920s to 15 years today. Just 15 years. At this rate, 75% of today's big companies, 75% of the names you know, won't be around in 2027."[9]

Because of these massive shifts in the job market, our kids are going to have to write their own stories. This will be difficult to do if they spend the majority of their childhood with someone else as the author.

When John Gatto writes on intellectual dependency, he describes "the millions of things of value to study."[10] This singular phrase compelled me to pause and make a shift in our homeschool. I'd thought that K–12 education was broad, but when I took a step back in light of Gatto's words, I realized that traditional education was much narrower than I'd originally believed. The illusion of educational depth and breadth for me came solely from the sheer amount of time kids spend in school throughout childhood. Not only are we talking about seven-plus hours a day, 180 days a year, for the majority of childhood, but we are also talking about the best hours of the day. The school system co-opts the time period when kids are most alert and eager and often sends them home tired.

All of this happens while leaving out "millions of things of value to study." Millions. Who decided what to keep and what to cut?

What I have found through our journey with our own kids over the years is that, through their personal areas of interest, they learn all sorts of things that would be included in a traditional curriculum. Instead of learning it systematically at predetermined grade levels, however, they learn it through the study of something that enthralls them.

## The Homeschooling Experience: A Case Study

Each educational philosophy book I read challenged me to change. This "millions of things of value to study" phrase was no exception. Did it truly make sense for me to orchestrate everything? To figure it out after the kids went to bed or in the summer months heading into a new school year? I was positioning myself as the expert, as the authority. I wasn't considering what each child brought to the table.

In *The War of Art*, Steven Pressfield describes children this way: "Each came into the world with a distinct and unique personality, an identity so set that you can fling stardust and great balls of fire at it and not morph it by one micro-dot.

Each kid was who he was. Even identical twins, constituted of the exact same genetic material, were radically different from Day One and always would be."[11]

Radically different. Not morph it by one micro-dot.

And yet we march each child through homogeneity. For most of their childhood.

So I introduced individual interests to our homeschool. Begrudgingly. And also midyear. Inconveniently, I hadn't read this passage at the beginning of September, but when I came across it in midwinter, I knew immediately that I needed to make a shift.

I gathered our children who were eight and older. I might've been influenced by Rudolf Steiner's definition of middle childhood as ages nine through twelve,[12] but our three oldest kids are less than three years apart, so I included the youngest of that trio, who was eight at the time.

With excitement in my voice and annoyance in my heart, I announced a new plan, called "individual interests," for the coming school year. I asked the kids to think about what they would want to study if they could pick anything in the world.

This is how our family became members of the Central Michigan Lapidary and Mineral Society.

For his individual interest, the youngest of the trio announced, "Rocks!" He was bright-eyed after spending a Michigan summer searching for Petoskey stones and Leland Blues along the shores of Lake Michigan. I faked enthusiasm. To me, rocks were boring. Though isn't this exactly the point? "Millions of things of value to study."

Would geology have ever come up throughout the K–12 course of study? Yes. Would I have put any emphasis on it at all? No.

After the kids chose their individual interests, I had to figure out how to give them opportunities to immerse themselves in their topics of choice. This rock pick overwhelmed me. Not only did I consider the topic boring, but I had no idea what I was going to do about finding resources for an eight-year-old.

But a little internet searching brought me to MichRocks .com and this club that we could join, not too far from our house. It met once a month and cost only $15 for an entire family to join for the year. This discovery was a game-changer. Despite our limited budget, MichRocks.com led us to a local club that offered not only affordability but also a treasure trove of educational opportunities. Our entire family could immerse ourselves in monthly gatherings that were rich, hands-on learning experiences.

There could be a wealth of inexpensive resources available to you as well—just a quick internet search away, waiting to enrich your homeschooling journey without straining your budget.

Far from being an emotional and logistical strain on me, finding resources to nurture our kids' interests turned out to be rather easy. I still have a picture of the notes I took when I was researching during this phase. I had written down from MichRocks.com that this club was for "anyone interested in rocks, geology and rockhounding."[13] Check. Check. Check. But these were different types of checkboxes than those found in a traditional curriculum. They were self-initiated rather than created by the state. Our family's engagement with the Central Michigan Lapidary and Mineral Society exemplifies turning theory into practice with our homeschooling approach.

When I think back to the first time we attended a meeting, I get teary because this turned out to be a remarkable answer for learning about geology, not just for our rocks kid but also for our entire family. I was changed as I saw firsthand how one phrase in one book could lead to so much life and growth.

As you might expect, when our family showed up at this first meeting, we were the youngest ones there. By far. I had a trepidatious first step over the threshold into the meeting room with a ten-, nine-, eight-, six-, and three-year-old in tow.

In my mind's eye, all I could imagine was bland. Boring. Lifeless. But this room was hustling and bustling. More than thirty adults were walking from table to table, pulling out their favorite types of rocks and showing them to others, who responded with expressions of delight. Oohs and aahs emanated from the room. We were drawn in, enraptured by the beauty of the earth just like the rest of the members.

Immediately, I saw that the value of this experience went far beyond learning about a simple topic. My mind began to whirl. Sure, we were clearly going to learn about rocks. There were rocks and books about rocks everywhere. All our kids were going to learn about rocks, not just the one who had the most interest, because we were there as a family.

But our kids were also going to learn about finding community. They were going to learn about the value of a hobby. They were going to learn people skills, including how to talk with those from an older generation. They were going to be surrounded by people who were committed to lifelong learning. There would be even greater rewards that I didn't realize yet.

Our kids slipped in seamlessly. They caught the buzzing energy of the room. Other members were surprised but tickled to see enthusiastic kids in the mix, and rock show-and-tell was off to the races. The air was filled with the hum of conversation. Our children scattered, finding their own way, creating their own experiences based on who and what caught their eye.

If just this one experience had cost $15, it would've felt worth it. We left wide-eyed, our view of the world expanded. And yet, there was so much more to come.

When the meeting was about to start, we were told that there was hot chocolate available . . . for free! I'm not sure where you live, but if you live in Michigan, hot chocolate is like gold in any season but the summer. Our kids were thrilled. They each made a hot chocolate, and we settled into our seats.

"Will they have hot chocolate each time we come, Mom?" They sure did.

There was a form to fill out. I handed it to our eight-year-old. (Add reading and handwriting to the list of skills we would work on that night!) The form included questions and prompts like, "Circle your interests/hobbies/talents," followed by the options of archaeology, fossils, fluorescents, mineralogy, photography, and twelve others, with a space to fill in another rock topic that pulled at your heartstrings. I added vocabulary and spelling to this cascading list in my mind about all we were learning. Our son circled collecting, carving, fossils, and geology.

This form included club functions. You could be a presenter or help with the newsletter. You could join the hospitality team or be a part of the rock show. *Rock show?!*

*What's that?* There was also an option to get a membership badge. This was getting better and better.

The meeting kicked off with some call-to-order type things. There was a beautiful formality to it. In all of this, our kids were being exposed to an adult world that didn't consist of Netflix and doomscrolling. They were seeing firsthand that there are perks of being an adult—namely, that you can still talk about rocks with others who love them too.

After some opening lines, new members got the opportunity to introduce themselves. *Are you kidding me?* I thought. In just ten minutes, we'd already gotten this host of benefits, and now we were adding public speaking to the mix! Our eight-year-old son stood up in front of an entire room of people, introduced himself, and told everyone where he was from. He introduced our family as well, and the president added, "This is their first meeting. New members," which was followed by a round of applause. Experiences like this are so affirming, helping people stand taller and feel more confident in the world.

At this particular meeting, there was also a rock-tumbling demonstration. Given the intense interest of the members, meetings cover a wide range of topics in depth. Rock tumbling involves different grit levels in order to get the rocks to truly shine. Throughout the course of one evening, we were learning about math, vocabulary, science, geography, and even career paths because the single topic of rock tumbling led to conversations about where the rocks were found, what geologists did for work (there were several in the club), and so on. The cross-curricular learning ran deep when we were learning in context.

When we reached the middle of the meeting, there was a snack break. I kid you not. These grown-ups had a snack time built into every society meeting. And because they weren't ragged mothers who had been up all night nursing or wiping little noses, the snacks were legitimately good. This was no table filled with bags of goldfish. It was more like a homemade bake sale where everything was free.

Beyond all of this—if you can even believe that there was more—our kids won prizes from a raffle, and once again these weren't piddly things a group of just-starting-out young moms might pull together. There was a tray with a whole host of prizes. There were games and exquisite rock crafts to choose from. We came home with a shark's tooth (nothing cooler if you're eight years old) and some fool's gold!

At the end of the night, we were given an additional packet of information about the society. Here we learned that each month there were door prizes. This club also had an extensive library filled with books, magazines, and videos that could be borrowed. The packet spoke of monthly demonstrations and presentations from experts, a yearly silent auction, and field trips. Several times a year, field trip opportunities would arise. These ranged from single-day outings to overnights in Michigan as well as out of state.

Five years later, our kids still reminisce about the year we joined the club. I asked our oldest daughter, who is now fourteen, about some of the things she remembers.

"I remember the hot chocolate. I remember one time there was an auction, and my bids won some of the things. I remember we always had the one specific table we went and sat at. I remember the first time we walked in and saw the

Yooperlites glowing. I remember getting all the prizes we won from the raffles. I still have them. That was really fun. I remember the walk up there into the building. I remember the guy with the glasses who would always call out the names of the people who won."

Our younger son also remembers the hot chocolate, but he told me just recently that, when we were out along the shores of the Great Lakes in Michigan, he would always look for the different types of rocks the presenters had taught him about at the monthly meetings. "I found a lot of them, Mom," he told me. "I was specifically looking for them."

The club was clearly a worthy part of our pursuit of education, but the story doesn't stop there.

## Self-Driven Learning Experiences

In one of our monthly meetings, the presenter introduced us to Yooperlites, a type of rock that had been discovered in Michigan's Upper Peninsula only a few years prior. Wow! Brand-new discoveries were still happening in the world of geology. That was exciting.

What makes Yooperlites special is that they glow bright purple and orange under a black light. In normal daylight, they look like any other rock. But when it's completely dark and you shine a black-light flashlight on them, they light up in brilliant ways, each rock slightly different from another. The presenter had also brought an entire bag of them to show everyone. This was jaw-dropping to see in person. When plain old gray rocks light up bright orange, everyone is entranced, no matter if you're super interested in rocks or not.

Two and half years later, we found ourselves in Michigan's stunning Upper Peninsula for an end-of-summer/kick-off-a-new-school-year celebration, and our kids brought up the Yooperlites. They remembered them after all that time. We didn't have any plans to do this on that particular vacation, but because the kids were excited about it, we decided to take the two-hour drive from where we were staying to the shores of Lake Superior, where these rocks are sometimes found. We hoped to find a small shop that sold black-light flashlights along the way. After checking two stores without any luck, we stopped at one last store in Grand Marais that was about to close. We ran in with bated breath, and there, right near the cash register, was a basket of black-light flashlights. We purchased a few to share and headed toward a rocky section of shoreline on Lake Superior.

This was at the end of August in Northern Michigan, and when the sun lowers over the horizon at that time of year, it starts to get cold. We had to wait until late to even start our search because it had to be completely dark to use the black lights. We also knew we had a two-hour drive back to our cottage awaiting us.

The sun dipped. The wind whipped. The waves crashed. Up and down the shoreline we walked, swinging our flashlights back and forth, back and forth. We looked and looked. Ten minutes. Twenty minutes. Thirty minutes. Our noses were starting to run. Our youngest was getting restless. Still nothing. Shivering and disappointed, we were about to call it a night when we heard some screaming coming from down the beach. It grew louder and louder. We began to make out the words.

"I found one! I found one!" our oldest daughter was shrieking.

That was, and still is, a highlight of our kids' entire child-hoods.

As everyone gathered around, she pointed her flashlight at this rock, and it lit up. We had seen these before, piled in a paper sack in a room at the rock club. But it was life-changing for our daughter to be outdoors, holding a Yooperlite that she found all on her own in the final minutes that we were going to be there.

"How did you find one?" we asked.

"I knew that it was getting cold and that everyone was ready to go home. I also knew that God controls the winds and the waves, so I asked him to help me find one, and then I looked down, and there it was."

This is an education.

It is an education that cannot be confined to four walls. It must be lived. It must seep into your being, into your pores, into your soul. It is created both in community and in solitude. It frames how you view the rest of your life, the rest of the world. It happens when you live your life in real places, with real people, learning the things that are outside of a textbook.

## Reflections and Forward Looking

When I reflect on our journey, it's clear that homeschooling is not just about education; it's about preparing for a life of continuous learning and adaptation. In embracing homeschooling, we embrace a more natural, integrated form of learning that prepares our children not just for tests but for life.

There are truly "millions of things of value to study." Archery and crochet. Origami and ballroom dance. Guitar and glassblowing. Creative writing and Yooperlites.

Slowly but surely, I was loosening the reins. I was dethroning myself. I was learning through living right alongside our kids.

As a homeschool family, you, too, are learning through living, and that includes both the high points and the low points. In my own days of doubt, I often come back to those words of John Holt that opened this chapter. Whose kids are living "fully and energetically and happily?" Yours are. Mine are. Homeschooled kids are.

Teacher Tom Hobson wrote, "I am comfortable knowing that children are learning because they are playing, and that's enough."[14] Indeed, it is enough.

Homeschool parent, you are doing it right. You are learning through living. By embracing this lifestyle, you're not just educating your children; you're giving them the tools to thrive in a constantly evolving world.

# 2

## You Are Allowing for Individual Timelines

Childhood is not a race to see how quickly a child can read, write and count. It is a small window of time to learn and develop at the pace that is right for each individual child. Earlier is not better.

—Magda Gerber[1]

I didn't teach our youngest daughter to read—and yet she knows how to read. And she can read well, at or above grade level. You may think this sounds irresponsible, or you may think it sounds genius. No matter your opinion, I will tell the story of how she learned to read stories without a teacher.

There is a book I read early on in my homeschooling years that I recommend to each and every parent who is considering homeschooling. I've already mentioned the author, John Holt, several times, and while I think all his books are good and insightful, the only one that I recommend to all is called *Learning All the Time: How Small Children Begin to Read, Write, Count, and Investigate the World, Without Being Taught.*

The book I own is tattered, filled with dog-eared pages and notes, and while I got a lot out of it, I always questioned the reading part. Sure, I saw that our children learned to count without being explicitly taught. Numbers are woven into everything from food to the page numbers of a book, to money, to the wheels on a bicycle. I saw my kids investigate the world without a single prompt. They loved searching for things like puffball mushrooms on local hikes. (These are elusive mushrooms that emit a little cloud of yellow smoke when you press on them like a button, earning them the nickname "fart mushrooms" or "wolf fart mushrooms.") I even saw how our kids might begin to write as they often copied older siblings and adults in the act of writing, though what actually landed on paper at first was tangled scribbles that amounted to gibberish.

But reading? How could a child possibly begin to read without being taught? I was puzzled, and I had major doubts that it could actually work, even though I had heard stories from others who knew someone who had learned on their own. Even knowing that my kids had already learned a tremendous amount on their own—and complex things at that—I still had a lot of skepticism.

Let me preface this chapter by saying it is about individualism. It's about the beauty of being able to structure a curriculum and a childhood around your unique son or daughter. I describe my approach and experience with reading solely to show that there are other paths that exist outside of kindergarten literacy. Students with dyslexia, for instance, may have their own timeline that works best for them. This may include some early interventions and support to help with long-term success. Or you may have a child who is keenly interested in learning how to read before kindergarten. The key with homeschooling is that you can allow for these individual timelines to exist.

Just as the previous chapter was about learning through living instead of through a narrow scope of prescribed subjects, this chapter is also about taking a more individualized approach to our children's education that will help them now and in the future.

## Dude Perfect

Dude Perfect is an American sports and comedy group. In our home, they are Coby, Tyler, Cody, Cory, and Garrett—a group of five friends who met in college and became famous via YouTube videos of "trick shots," different types of sports shots that seem almost impossible to make but that this group of guys would make over and over again, film, and then put on YouTube.

Our kids were introduced to Dude Perfect by some friends, and their interest grew quickly to the point where we were planning a Dude Perfect–themed birthday party for our oldest daughter. One of the party games was called "Wheel Unfortunate," an activity that is woven here and there throughout the Dude Perfect YouTube videos. Reminiscent of *Wheel of Fortune*, this game involves a giant wheel split into different-colored triangles. Instead of having dollar amounts or the devastating "Lose a Turn" on them, each slice of this wheel has something unfortunate, like swim with gators, sleep in sand, pierce your ear with a fishhook, and drive until your car runs out of gas. One of the Dude Perfect five is chosen at random to spin the wheel. Wherever it lands, the response is always the same: "That's unfortunate!"

For our party adaptation, we used a smaller wheel and mixed in prizes with random items like a fork or an egg. Our plan was to write each of the guests' names on slips of paper and draw them out of a hat to announce when their turn was up. All our kids sat around the table, slips of paper ready, and we began to write, fold the papers, and put them in the hat.

At the time, our youngest was four. She had never written anything legible up to that point, though she had spent a lot of time developing her fine motor skills through coloring and playing outside. We talked about letters often, as her interest had been piqued, and she often pointed out a W or an E on signs and in books. We had a little song about the letters in her name that we sang while she brushed her teeth.

On this day, she sat and watched as name after name went into the hat, and then she grabbed a slip of paper and wrote her name out, plain as day.

No one had ever taught her how.

John Holt talks often about the inner drives that we have. Why would a baby who is fully taken care of ever attempt to roll over, crawl toward something, or try to feed themselves? Because as they grow, they begin to observe what those around them are doing, and they gradually learn the purposes of their own movements and growth. Rolling over changes their perspective. Crawling allows for mobility. A prized toy out of reach provides motivation.

Babies watch intently as your mouth forms words. They observe human speech and develop a broader understanding that speaking enables communication. A young child can say "Up" to let Mommy or Daddy know they want to be held. With language comes the power of expression.

My skepticism about reading and writing as subjects that might be self-taught came from my own preconceived notions that learning to read and write were tedious, laborious, and unenjoyable. A society that bemoans literacy scores and has all sorts of early intervention literacy programs had left this impression on my mind. There was no way that learning to read and write could be as seamless and child-driven as learning to walk—at least, that was my assumption.

And yet, here was my four-year-old writing with nary a lesson. She wanted her name on that slip of paper, so she wrote it. And then, without prompting, she took the entire pile of paper scraps and wrote her name again and again and again. She grabbed more paper, cut some wonky-looking strips, and continued to write her name. Practice. Repeat. The steps for mastery emerging from her own small hand.

Over the next year, she continued to write on strips of paper. In her mind she had married writing with that particular material. Sometimes her strips of paper would say "mommy." Sometimes "hug." Often "I love you."

I've kept those scraps. They carry a lot of meaning. They are small tokens that remind me of child capacity and the value of aiming to make something enticing instead of forcibly teaching it. And maybe we don't have to do that much. Maybe the world is enticing enough on its own and doesn't need our help.

Interestingly, John Holt goes as far as reminding the child of their inner capacity. We so often do the opposite. As the adults, we take over. But listen to how he frames it: "We could make it clear to the children that writing is an extension of powers *they already have, and that they got for themselves*: namely, the power of speech. We should constantly remind them that they figured out for themselves how to understand and talk like all the bigger people around them, and that learning to write and to read is easy."[2]

Dr. Peter Gray puts it this way in *Mother Nature's Pedagogy*: "Children come into the world biologically designed to educate themselves."[3] He goes on to say, "Children are brilliant learners because they don't think of themselves as learning; they think of themselves as doing."[4]

In his book *Free to Learn*, Gray describes babies' quest to learn about their world without being instructed to do so, which is evident at birth. "Within hours of their births, infants begin to look longer at novel objects than at those they have already seen." In fact, studying babies allows scientists to assess an infant's ability to form memories. "Babies who look significantly longer at a new pattern or object than at one they have already seen must perceive the difference between the two and must, at some level, remember having seen the old one before."[5]

Back to what I said about individualism—reading may not be easy for each and every child. But for many, it will be. And if it's not reading, there will be some subject matter that comes easily. What a vote of confidence we would give a child if we continuously and constantly remind them of all they've already learned on their own.

## The Path to Full Literacy

It was the strips of paper that gave me the confidence to step out of the teacher role when it came to reading. I might never have done this if we'd had fewer children, but I had already used the book *Teach Your Child to Read in 100 Easy Lessons* for our first four kids and knew it was a fail-safe sitting on our counter if I ultimately decided to pick it up again.

What is the plan when you're attempting to allow your child to learn to read on their own timeline? There isn't much of one. It's similar to the plan you make when they're about to start walking. You support them on their own timeline, whenever they are ready.

In a homeschool, this readiness is evident when the child shows interest in reading. Having a lot of books around the house, spending a lot of time at the library, and reading to yourself and your child subtly show the value of this skill. Fill your home with a variety of reading materials. Grab them at garage sales or library sales. Books, magazines, comics, and even newspapers will cater to different interests and reading levels. Create a cozy reading nook if you have the space. Get your hands on anything that fascinates your child. Does she love bugs? Does he love monster trucks? You could even place little stations of favorite-themed items around your home for kids to find as they go throughout the day.

Most children love to be read to. They love stories and adventure, yet inevitably, there will be times when a parent won't be able to read to them at the exact moment they want a story. There are times when you are out in public and a child may want to be able to read a sign or a menu at a restaurant. Slowly but surely, the internal motivation increases.

They want what they see others have. And so they begin to ask questions. They may ask, "What is this word?" and little by little you find yourself sounding out sounds and explaining simple rules of phonetics. Just like learning to crawl or learning to walk, the progress is slow but steady, with a fair number of mishaps.

And then one day, as in my case, you glance over and your child, who you never formally taught to read, is reading a Berenstain Bears book or a Little Critter book, and your jaw drops. It actually worked.

But it didn't happen at age five. For us, it happened at age seven. For others, it might be ten. The Alliance for Childhood put out a report stating, "No research documents long-term gains from learning to read in kindergarten," and the greater gains are clearly seen when young kids have access to "active, play-based experiences."[6]

When you do a deep dive into different research studies about how kids learn, it is remarkable how these jargony articles basically point to play as helping with many facets of development. For example, one study of visuomotor skills and academic achievement explains, "As researchers examine the cognitive and behavioral skills involved in early academic achievement, new research suggests that components of fine motor skills play an important role in facilitating the learning process. . . . Better VMS could aid behavioral SR and EF by freeing cognitive resources, allowing the child to divide attention between tasks that require visual and motor skills."[7] In this study, SR stands for self-regulation and EF stands for executive function. In other words, the visuomotor skills that children begin to develop at birth will help them academically and beyond. Visuomotor skills are involved in all the simple things that kids are driven to do on their own when they have the right materials handy, like building with blocks, scribbling on paper, throwing and catching a ball, and cutting with scissors. That chunk of bangs that your three-year-old just cut off is part of the learning process.

Behavioral self-regulation and executive function, combined with these visuomotor skills, are related to math, emergent literacy, and vocabulary scores. Simple play experiences drive so much of child development.

We don't have to control learning so much. We don't have to control the timeline, and we don't have to control the outcome. Strict measures of comprehension are not the end goal, according to Holt, who writes, "For children reading (or adults, for that matter), the most important thing is *not* that they should understand all of what they read. . . . What is important is that children should enjoy their reading enough to want to read more."[8]

More strips of paper. More books. More experiences. More of what we love. These lead to all kinds of learning, not just the linear kind.

It is understandable to be nervous about this type of approach, especially at the beginning. Additionally, different states require varying levels of documentation in regard to homeschooling. Informal assessments such as portfolios, records of family projects, and reflective journals offer a holistic view of a child's development. It is important to have a clear understanding of local homeschooling laws and regulations. Each state or country can have different requirements for subjects taught, hours of instruction, and recordkeeping, and these can vary over time due to changing regulations. Connect with local homeschooling associations for a rundown of legal requirements.

## Our Own Learning Time Frames

I learned how to bake bread as an adult. Some learn when they're three.

I learned how to embroider when I was an adult. Some learn when they're nine.

We often celebrate people in adulthood when they finally pursue a passion or learn something they'd always dreamed of. We say that it's never too late. Except when it comes to that K–12 timeline.

There is nothing inherently wrong with attempting to learn things on a predetermined timeline, but it is not uncommon for these timelines to leave lifelong stigmas. The number of high school students who walked into my classroom and told me they weren't good at math was staggering. Furthermore, it wasn't true. What was true was that they usually struggled in one or two areas (often fractions, which are much harder to conceptualize and manipulate than counting numbers), and their lack of understanding seeped into newer topics, so they felt forever lost.

I made it my personal mission to help remove those stigmas. I often said things like, "Well, look at that. It turns out you weren't bad at math at all. You just didn't understand this one thing." Sometimes it worked. Sometimes it didn't. The things we come to believe about ourselves when we are young are deeply ingrained.

As we worked through these teens' learning gaps, I heard story after story of frustrated teachers who had ridiculed them when they didn't understand (or at least they perceived they were being ridiculed). They spoke of being too embarrassed to ask questions out of a fear of snippy remarks from other students or even the teacher. One student told me that her ninth-grade teacher said she would never be good at math, in front of the entire classroom of kids.

Quite often, these kids were going home to parents who threw up their hands as well. They carried the same stigmas. A childhood friend of mine, who is a successful chef and can cater anything from a one-year-old's birthday party to an event with hundreds of people, told me she never understood fractions until she began cooking as an adult. "Why didn't anyone present them to me this way?" she wondered. She was convinced that if she had learned about fractions in the context of cooking, she wouldn't have struggled so deeply. But what school can take the things a child is already interested in and use that as a vessel for teaching mathematical concepts? A homeschool can.

One of the hardest things about the homeschool journey is fearing the unknown ahead. Learning about the experiences of others who had childhoods that didn't unfold on a prescribed timeline gave me more resolve.

I had a conversation with Dr. Carla Hannaford for our *1000 Hours Outside Podcast*.[9] She has earned a PhD and influenced countless numbers of kids and families around the world with her studies. We talked about her book *Smart Moves: Why Learning Is Not All in Your Head*, which is one of my all-time favorite parenting books. She opened the conversation by talking about her own childhood. She let me know that she didn't read until she was ten years old. Imagine that! Consider a child today who goes all the way through kindergarten, first, second, and third grade without the ability to read. How would that child emerge from the public school system? Would they have an innate view of themselves as smart and competent?

In bygone days, there wasn't as strict an adherence to timelines for learning objectives. "It didn't really matter back then," Carla said. She is currently in her eighties and would've been ten in the early 1950s. Following the timeline of the child, mirroring Dr. Hannaford's childhood experience, allows for the customization of educational content to meet their needs. If a child struggles with a specific subject, more time and resources can be devoted to it, unlike in a traditional school setting where the class must move at a collective pace. Conversely, less time can be given to learning that comes easily to a child, opening up more hours in the day for other pursuits.

Our oldest son, who is in the middle of his high school years, recently started an internship in a field of study that he is enamored with. In the interview process, no one asked him what age he learned to read. The fact that he didn't learn to read until age seven had no bearing on his employability or his performance. It didn't matter.

Not only will no one ask our children at what age they learned to read, but no one will ask who taught them. Being self-taught is something that will hardly come up, if ever, in the entire course of life . . . unless you end up writing a book about it, like I'm doing.

Early anything may come with a few bragging rights for the parents, but it's not long-lasting. When you're sitting around the sports complex for your daughter's 12U volleyball game, no one is going to care that she learned to read when she was three and a half. Bragging rights are short-lived and not worth pursuing at the expense of your child's view of themselves. If early learning is self-initiated, run with it. If learning comes later than expected, run with that too.

And certainly, when your child becomes an adult, they aren't ever going to enter a conversation leading with early-childhood milestones that they conquered. If you talk much about early-childhood accomplishments as a grown adult, you just sound weird. If I kick off a conversation with "Hi, I'm Ginny. I learned how to read when I was four, before I even started kindergarten," I'm not winning myself any friends.

## An Eye Toward the Future

Beyond the stigmas we can attach to children when we set timelines for skills mastered, how do current methods of teaching kids translate into adulthood? Childhood is, or should be, a beautiful blend of soaking in the present with an eye toward the future. In this era, the future is on the move. The landscape of job opportunities is shifting. This is exciting and daunting at the same time. However, the model of milestone checking doesn't prepare our kids for this kind of future.

A straight-line, stepping-stone approach only works well if we know what we're stepping toward. And we don't. In the past, the stepping stones would have pointed to a thirty-year career in the same company, working up the ranks, and then retiring at fifty-five with a pension and health care. But the final outcome has changed, so these stepping stones don't work anymore. In many cases, they are taking kids completely off course, depositing them in a place that doesn't exist anymore.

Today's kids will be career pivoters, often several times. A straight and narrow timeline approach to childhood growth doesn't lay a foundation for the ability to morph and change, to branch off and out of a prescribed path.

Sure, schools and teachers try to help kids prepare. Most teachers have big hearts. They view their kids as individuals. They get to know them and love them over the course of a school year. It is the constraints of space, time, and practicality that create an environment where kids cannot flourish and bloom when they are ready. It simply cannot work at scale.

I taught a basic math class one year at a public high school in Farmington, Michigan. This was a class full of kids who wore the "I'm not good at math" badge (figuratively, obviously).

My sixth-hour basic math class was held in a half room of sorts. It was an odd shape. It didn't have that expansive feel that some classrooms do, with large windows opening to a view of the playground or nearby woods. The room had no windows, and it was separated from another room with one of those foldable accordion walls, creating a shape that felt like an expanded hallway rather than a classroom.

This expanded hallway with no windows housed myself and thirty-six kids who wore "I'm not good at math" badges. *Thirty-six kids?*

Yes, that's correct. The reason the number was so high was because of another math teacher who also taught basic math during sixth hour. She was down the hall and to the right. She was a tenured teacher in our math department and had been awarded Teacher of the Year in our district at least once, possibly more, though my memory is a little foggy. She had won a car. That much I knew.

Her class—the exact same class in the exact same time slot—had a size that numbered in the teens. *How could that be? Why not divvy it up a little better?* you might think.

Well, on a regular basis, the principal or vice principal of the school would show up at the door of my oddly shaped classroom, *during* class, and knock. I would open the door to find said administrator standing there with a teen. "The other teacher won't take this student. Will you?"

*Is that allowed?* I thought. Teaching surely would be easier if we could just pick and choose who we wanted to teach. Was this how you get to become Teacher of the Year and win a car?

Of course I would take the student. "It's a little crowded in here, but come on in!"

In those days, I was still a newer teacher learning the ropes. One thing I learned early on is that many students in Michigan had Individualized Education Plans (also called IEPs) that were legal documents under US law, written for students with disabilities, that would outline ways the school district could help a student succeed. I loved that this was part of the system because it gave extra support when needed. I often sat in on meetings with parents, counselors, and even attorneys to find creative ways to help kids make it through their classes.

An IEP might say that a student would need their notes written for them. Check! Our notes for each class were always preprinted, fill-in-the-blank style, and students with IEPs could get a copy with the blanks already filled in. An IEP might require that I wear a headset microphone and that the sound be amplified through speakers in the room. Check!

63

No problem. There were lots of other ways to accommodate different learning styles and needs, like having extra time for tests, tests being read to students, and completing half of the homework problems.

In this particular basic math class, however, more than 50% of the students had IEPs. This would have been no problem, except that each plan required that the student have a front-row seat in the classroom, and there weren't enough front-row seats.

Teachers and administrators understand the value of individualization. Yet in practical terms, it's simply not possible. For the sake of practicality, we land on an approach that has the look and feel of an assembly line.

Since childhood education isn't only about the here and now, we must ask: What do we implicitly teach kids when we orchestrate life this way?

The question my children get asked the most by adults, by far, is what grade they are in. Kids are defined by school structures from the get-go. I'm always surprised by the question and wonder why adults don't ask the similar yet in some ways totally different question, "How old are you?"

Justin Whitmel Earley talks about how the introductory question in first conversations and new relationships used to be, "Who is your family?" In his book *Made for People*, he writes, "This movement of work to the center of our identities has not made us very happy. Working is now a leading indicator of identity in America."[10] So what is the leading indicator of identity for kids in America? Grade level? Ironically, homeschooled kids (and their parents) often don't know the answer to this question, which starts an introductory conversation on awkward footing.

In the short term, prescriptive timelines can be stifling and even damaging. In the long term, they just don't set kids up for adulthood. Adulthood has no timelines. The timelines that used to be more prevalent have vanished, so people are losing their way.

Think about this logically. If thirteen of your formative years are spent with authority figures dictating a majority of the steps you should take for your growth, and then you walk across a stage wearing a strange hat and a robe so someone can hand you a rolled scroll signifying that portion of your life is over, and the authority figures who coaxed you along a prescribed path with kids exactly your age suddenly disappear, would you be well prepared to figure out what's next for you in a world that is changing quickly? There is so much to unpack there.

You didn't own many of your decisions up to that point. Now you own them all. You were raised in a group setting. Now you're an individual out on your own.

So often, it feels like we are transitioning from a straight-timeline approach in childhood to the corporate-ladder approach in adulthood. Why is every approach so linear and rigid? Where are the paint splatters? The noodles? The winding trails through the meadows?

Joy Marie Clarkson compares and contrasts the corporate ladder to a mountain in her book *You Are a Tree*. It gave me a lot to think about.

On a ladder, you can go only up or down. On a mountain, there are an infinite number of directions you can go.

On a ladder, success is only at or near the top. On a mountain, you will find joy in many places. You might find it when the trees break and you can see a majestic view for miles. You might find it in a pristine lake you come across. You might find it in the wildlife you see, the sunlight that warms your skin, or the company you are with.

On a ladder, your position is shaky. People are clawing at you from the bottom and kicking at your fingers from the top. The people below you want to be above you, and the people above you want to maintain their position. On a mountain, your foundation is secure. There's enough room for everyone to be successful and happy.

On a ladder, the top rung isn't safe. In fact, ladders have stickers on the top step that tell you not to step on it. It's not that the top step is poorer quality than the others, but it is less safe. At the top, it's very easy to topple. On a mountain, you don't even have to get to the top to say that your journey was a success.

Clarkson says it this way: "When it comes to a mountain, the top is not always the best place to be; it is bright, un-shielded, exposed to the elements."[11]

A meandering success is more realistic, more stable, and more enjoyable. It allows others to come around you. On a ladder, you're alone on your rung, fighting to maintain your position or climb over the person above you.

So far, you are on a roll! Simply by choosing home education, you are learning so much through living, and you are allowing for individual timelines and all the benefits that accompany a personalized education and childhood.

Catering to your individual child in your home helps them avoid lifelong stigmas, prepares a foundation for a future with endless possibilities, and communicates to them that they are known and loved.

Homeschool parent, you are doing it right. What a beautiful and effective way to learn and to grow throughout childhood. This lays the foundation to continue learning and following individual paths into adulthood.

# 3

# You Are Leaving Space for Boredom

Let children experience boredom; there is nothing healthier for a child than to learn how to use their own interior resources to work through the challenges of being bored.

—Nicholas Kardaras, *Glow Kids*[1]

Before I became a mother, I was a public school teacher. Before I was a public school teacher, I was a substitute teacher. Before I was a substitute teacher, I taught swim lessons, lifeguarded, taught piano lessons, tutored math, and was the big rat at Chuck E. Cheese. I like kids. Clearly.

When I got the call to substitute teach for a kindergarten classroom, I felt like I had reached the pinnacle of existence. This was back in the day when kindergarten was split in two by lunch. You fell into one of two camps: a.m. or p.m. I was an a.m. kindergarten kid. We got up and got to it, and we were done with our circle time, play stations around the classroom, recess, and goodbye hugs by lunch. Then we walked home. The p.m. kids seemed like a wild breed. What did they do all morning? Their day wrapped up close to dinnertime. I would imagine that most years, those kindergarten teachers would have a slightly favorite group, depending on the mix of kids that year.

Those days are long gone. Kindergarteners joined their older grade-school counterparts en masse before 2010, and while there are a few exceptions for parents who can drive their child to the one school in their district that still offers a half-day kindergarten, a full day of school for five- and six-year-olds is now commonplace.

My substitute teaching experience occurred before this big shift. My whole body anticipated spending time with fifty or so five-year-olds, twenty-five in the morning and another twenty-five in the afternoon. When you have toddlers and babies, kindergarteners seem so old. They can match socks and take their plate to the sink. But from the viewpoint of a school that is filled with five- to eleven-year-olds, kindergarteners seem like babies. They show up with their baby teeth, and the transformation that occurs in one year ushers them from little kids to big kids. It's a remarkable change from kindergarten to first grade.

Having taught many older children, I was ready for the sweet little faces of both the a.m. and p.m. groups. Little did I know my anticipation would be short-lived. In fact, I would never, ever return to a kindergarten classroom again. By the end of the day, I was disheveled and exhausted, feeling as though I had lost a battle.

The first thing I noticed when I arrived for the school day was the substitute plans. For older children, the plans are fairly loose. Usually it was "watch a movie." Most of my substitute teaching days were spent babysitting kids who were old enough to be babysitters themselves.

Kindergarten was different. These plans were not loose. I'm surprised the teacher even had the capacity to write them out. Often when you call for a substitute, it's because you are sick. Not sniffle sick but on-death's-door sick. When you miss a day in the classroom, things snowball. Teachers don't miss too much. It's one thing to leave sub plans that say, "Watch *Searching for Bobby Fischer* and have the students write a paragraph about what they learned." Anyone could write those plans, even in the ICU. But these kindergarten plans were different. Wildly different.

First, they were not short. I was actually flipping pages to get from the beginning to the end. And there were a lot of words squeezed into those pages. Mind you, this was for a half day of school.

Second, the plans were extremely detailed and exacting. This was a minute-by-minute schedule of how the half day for these kids was going to run. I was going to have to keep this comprehensive document with me at all times if I had even a remote chance of keeping up with the plans.

I derailed within five minutes.

Of course, the teacher had left such comprehensive plans to help, to reduce chaos. But these kids had so much to tell me! Their tooth was wiggly. They needed help tying a shoe. They wanted to tell me about their favorite ice cream flavor and their favorite color and the name of their favorite cousin. This has a domino effect because once one child hears another talking about favorites, they are compelled to also share. I was thirteen minutes into the day and hadn't even gotten to the circle time song, which was supposed to take the first three minutes. Technically, I was sixteen minutes behind.

The rest of the day was a blur. I barely survived. But I've always remembered that minute-by-minute schedule. It made sense to have it because chaos would ensue otherwise. I know. I was there. But I always wondered about the benefits for the classroom as a whole versus the costs to the individual child. This intense structure in kindergarten is a product of broader changes in educational settings over the years, but our family's kindergarten year at home looked vastly different from what I experienced that day. Ours was entirely open-ended. There wasn't even a hint of a regimented schedule like the one I described. And yet, despite not having every minute filled, our kids have gone on to flourish.

We often structure childhood without considering the individual needs of each child. The one. The unique person who has so much to offer the world, even with a mouthful of baby teeth. Children need time to become themselves, but starting at an extremely young age, they are shuffled through a regimen that they didn't choose. They get no input whatsoever, and yet every day they attempt to align themselves with an approach that is good for a roomful of peers.

In a more natural environment—say, outside or in your home where there is more freedom—five-year-olds have the innate capacity to structure their own time. They find things of value that seem interesting and worthwhile to them and allocate some of their own childhood to those things. There is a tremendous upside here. Certainly, we value inquisitiveness and being a self-starter. These skills provide benefits well beyond the schooling years. But as with just about everything, there are pros and cons. The cons of open-ended time include things like mess, mayhem, and the two dreaded words "I'm bored."

## Boredom Is Not Failure

Somehow, the words "I'm bored" have become unbearable to parents. So I will begin with the words of Kim John Payne, Luis Fernando Llosa, and Scott Lancaster in their book *Beyond Winning*. They state it plainly. "When our children are bored, we have not failed them."[2]

Scribble that on a Post-it note and stick it on your bathroom mirror. Pen it in calligraphy on a sheet of paper and stick it on your fridge. Write it with a Sharpie on the wall in the toy room. Tattoo it on your wrist. The daily pressures of parenting drive us to need this ten-word reminder often.

This is not how things used to be. You can learn a lot more about the changes in society and how we ended up in this adult-directed child-rearing age in my book *Until the Streetlights Come On*. Without even going into the details of the whens and the whys, we feel this underlying pressure as parents to be the ones out in front, leading the parade, orchestrating the extracurriculars, filling each and every second with some developmental activity or another.

Mothers used to lock their kids out of the house *all summer long*.

Can you even imagine?

These days, such a parenting approach would be looked upon with scorn, disdain, and a side helping of deep judgment. A parent who doesn't "parent" at all hours of the day

73

might even be seen as neglectful. And while I can understand where this attitude comes from (and how it affects a parent's feelings of self-worth), research does not support adult-directed childhoods as a superior approach.

Of all the books I've read on play-based childhoods, *Balanced and Barefoot* by Angela Hanscom says it best:

> As adults, we may always feel that we know what is best for our children. A child's neurological system begs to differ. Children with healthy neurological systems naturally seek out the input they need on their own. They determine how much, how fast, and how high works for them at any given time. They do this without even thinking about it. If they are spinning in circles, it's because they need to. If they are jumping off a rock over and over, it is because they are craving that sensory input. They are organizing their senses through practice and repetition.[3]

Turns out that the lock-your-kids-outside-all-summer mothers were onto something. They weren't neglectful. There was, at some point, a baseline trust in the "child's neurological system." That's what we've lost.

Boredom gives kids opportunities to "seek out the input they need on their own." Without open spaces in the day, a child will have no chance to act upon their inner drive.

Boredom is not failure. Boredom is a springboard. It is a catalyst. It is gold. It is where the good stuff comes from. It is exciting. It represents endless possibilities. Boredom is a gift we hand to our children. It is the foundation of delight and discovery. Boredom is where we fall in love with painting, with music, with lying in the grass and watching the clouds float by, with life.

When days are packed minute by minute, hour by hour with "good" things, we forget about everything else that is wonderful and worthwhile outside of our rigid schedules.

This reality is actually freeing because, despite your best efforts, replicating the achievements of kindergarten teachers is impossible. Your job description as a homeschool parent includes being not only the teacher but also the lunch lady, recess attendant, janitor, curriculum coordinator, bus driver, specialist, counselor, researcher, and occasionally the principal. Classroom teachers are required to get a certain number of continuing education credits to maintain their certification. You are required to continue your education in order to survive. Additionally, you are the social life coordinator. This is a hefty role because it may mean that you are inviting others into your home that is trashed because the janitor is overworked (or sick, or nursing a baby, or all of the above).

You are in charge of purchasing all the school supplies, and depending on where you live and what your life circumstances are, you may have sacrificed an entire income to do so. Also, where are you going to put all those first-grade resources? How are you going to organize them? Are you going to keep them for when your three-year-old turns seven?

A school classroom contains the manipulatives, books, and hands-on materials for one grade (maybe two, if it's a split). At some point, your home may house everything that is needed for thirteen grades.

Try as you may, it's not possible to schedule your life in as regimented a way as you might like. You can have beautiful rhythms to your days, weeks, months, and years, but your life will never be timed to the minute. There will be more wiggle room than you feel comfortable with.

So, have you written it down yet? Have you nailed it on a post in your yard?

"When our children are bored, we have not failed them."

## Strategies for Embracing Boredom at Home

When our kids come to us bemoaning their boredom, as we know they will, we have two battles to fight. You've already won one. It's on your tattoo. You know this is good for them. You know it will bolster their interior resources. You are helping them dig a deep well for their future self. You are allowing for deep, deep roots that they will draw on for a lifetime. You've won one battle, though you may need to remind yourself of it from time to time.

In considering how best to meet individual developmental needs, we must also address the modern challenges that distract from them. Glennon Doyle succinctly captures the dilemma we face in this digital age when she says, "I find myself worrying most that when we hand our children phones, we steal their boredom from them. As a result, we are raising a generation of writers who will never start writing, artists who will never start doodling, chefs who will never make a mess of the kitchen, athletes who will never kick a ball against the wall, musicians who will never pick up their aunt's guitar and start strumming."[4]

While Doyle focuses on screen usage, there are so many ways we can fill our time that impede natural curiosity. Truly, I remind myself often that blank space is okay, and you may need to as well.

"May" isn't a strong enough word. You *will* need to have an inner voice or an outer voice from a friend that says,

"Those five hours when you laid on the couch because of _____ were not only okay, they were good." Or "Those three hours you spent at the park while you read an absorbing novel and your child dug in the dirt were not only okay, they were exceptional for development." Do you see the delight in your child's eyes? That span of time offered so much. To everyone.

Boredom is not only good for the child, it is also good for you as the homeschool parent. In generations gone by, kids knew what to do with themselves because less existed to entertain them on a regular basis. Extracurricular activities and travel sports were less time-consuming. Families had less expendable income. Many had only one vehicle. The television had nothing to blare. Childhood meant boredom. And kids knew how to handle it.

A child who can handle boredom benefits everyone in their surroundings as well as themselves. Creative kids are fun to play with, benefiting siblings, cousins, and neighbor kids. Innovative kids provide parents with a little reprieve here and there. In the long term, the entrepreneurial, self-starter type paves the way for the careers of others—a form of charity.

The thirteenth-century Jewish philosopher Moses Maimonides listed and ranked eight forms of charity. The lowest rung of the ladder is "When donations are given grudgingly." Just above that tier is giving cheerfully but less than we should. Next up, giving after being asked, then giving before being asked. The next three forms involve anonymity. These lead to the very highest form of charity, which is enabling the recipient to become self-reliant.[5]

Our oldest son is on the cusp of adulthood. As the oldest of five children within an eight-year span, he has spent much of his childhood directing his time. This was rooted in necessity rather than preference on my part, and yet as the years have ticked by, I've begun to see that what I deemed less than ideal has actually been life-giving. Recently, he started an internship at a small company that is owned by a young man in his early twenties who was homeschooled. Our son is learning skills that he's extremely interested in while earning a little money on the side. Maimonides would have considered the owner of this small company to be giving the highest form of charity. Business owners have the opportunity to enable others to become self-reliant in a multitude of ways.

Learning to follow the guidance of what's inside of us takes time and practice. A child who spends a majority of childhood on a minute-by-minute timeline, determined by adults, has less opportunity to develop the skills needed to engage with self and others.

Michaeleen Doucleff puts it this way in *Hunt, Gather, Parent*: "It's a lifelong skill to understand the situation around you and then know what to do."[6] Learning to understand the situations around us involves just that: learning. Constant direction does not give way to a deep understanding of our surroundings.

King Solomon said it this way:

> Go to the ant, you sluggard;
>> consider its ways and be wise!
> It has no commander,
>> no overseer or ruler,
> yet it stores its provisions in summer
>> and gathers its food at harvest. (Prov. 6:6–8)

If wise living includes the ability to act without a commander, providing space for boredom is the antithesis of failing.

We may worry that too much unstructured time could lead to unproductive or even risky behaviors. While this is a valid concern, over time when children are given the freedom to explore their interests, especially when passive screen use is unavailable, they develop more advanced problem-solving skills and creativity. If this is all new for you, a little supervision and gentle guidance can ensure that this time is used effectively without stifling independence.

## How to Actually Handle Boredom

You've won the first battle. You are convinced. "When our children are bored, we have not failed them." (Repeated over and over again, this statement is a beautiful reminder.)

But what does this actually look like in your home, when you're tending to your baby or cooking a meal and your children are whining, complaining, cajoling, and wailing about their boredom?

My body responds to this on a physical level. I feel it. My blood pressure starts to rise like a helium balloon that has escaped from its string. I begin to feel irritated. And panicked. You may start to feel angry or resentful.

No matter the feelings that arise, at least I no longer second-guess myself about the validity of boredom.

That's a lie. I do. So I refer back to what I know to be true.

The second battle is "What now?" Knowing that boredom is good for kids doesn't fix the immediate problem of your potentially spiraling feelings and a child who is unoccupied.

I asked our middle son what he does when he feels bored. He said, "Go bug my parents." It's his go-to. But we are busy with the many roles we've taken on as home-educating parents, so being bugged doesn't mesh well with everything else that needs to be accomplished in a day.

To begin with, employ every tactic you can possibly think of to remain calm (or return to calm if your calmness has floated away). Maybe you never learned any tactics. No worries! There are some amazing books with all sorts of ideas for you. *Stress Resets: How to Soothe Your Body and Mind in Minutes* by Dr. Jennifer Taitz is filled with "75 scientifically proven ways to improve how you respond to stress, both in the moment and the long run."[7] So grab a few ideas from this book. Learning to remain or return to calm is a beautiful skill to master, and we can thank our bored, whiny, clingy homeschooled children for helping us learn it. I'm partial to the idea of dunking your face in a bowl of ice for thirty seconds. This is easy, accessible, and silly. "A jolt of cold disrupts thinking and leaves you feeling refreshed," Taitz tells us.[8] More importantly, as we find ways that work for us and allow our bodies to return to a feeling of homeostasis, we are subsequently giving our kids tools as well.

Sissy Goff and David Thomas from Daystar Counseling Ministries and the *Raising Boys & Girls* podcast also have books with practical ideas for sinking into calm. They tout the strategy of box breathing, sometimes more excitingly called combat breathing.

*Raising Emotionally Strong Boys* by David Thomas is such a favorite book of ours that we own two copies—one for me and one for my husband, Josh. In it, David offers the phenomenal idea of using a product like an Apple Watch to monitor your blood pressure coming down in real time while applying different calm-down techniques. He says,

> I wear an Apple watch and will have boys take a look at my heart rate before the breathing starts and again once it ends. Consistently I can lower my heart rate with only a few minutes of combat breathing. This serves as hard evidence of the benefit any of us can experience in mastering these skills that can be used anywhere, anytime. I have boys use it before a timed test, in the dugout, on the free throw line, before a fine arts performance, when asking a girl to a dance, or during a hard conversation with parents. The benefits are endless.[9]

I have it on good authority from David that we can employ these skills as parents too, when our children are clawing at our legs or refusing to sleep or yowling about having nothing to do. Even better, we can revel in these trying situations because we are growing right alongside our children. "Regulation," David writes, "is some of the most important emotional work we can do as adults to position ourselves to model and teach this to the kids we love. We can only take the kids we love as far as we've gone ourselves."[10]

Sissy Goff repeated a similar sentiment when I spoke with her. "Until we can get healthy as families, no one is going to be that healthy individually," she said.[11]

As you deal with your kids' feelings of boredom that arise during a typical homeschool day, consider it a chance to do some inner work. View it as a growth opportunity for yourself. It is. When I spoke with Michaeleen Doucleff, author of *Hunt, Gather, Parent*, she described aiming to be less angry overall. Easier said than done. However, she did warn that "once you already have anger in your body, it is really hard to suppress it." She went on to say, "Every time you use your anger emotion, your brain wants to choose it again." Anger doesn't accomplish what we want it to. Michaeleen advocates for "finding a calmer emotion."[12] If this is something you struggle with, give yourself opportunities to practice. Truthfully, you won't even have to give yourself opportunities because your children will lovingly offer those up. In time, I learned firsthand that not only could I control my response, but my response could also deeply affect the outcome. Over the span of days, weeks, months, and years, your reactions become sort of second nature, and the ambiance of your home can radiate peace.

The *Love and Logic* books by Jim Fay (and other contributors) consistently advise using a tone of voice that is empathetic and caring. From the *Parenting with Love and Logic*[13] and *Teaching with Love and Logic*[14] books, I learned years ago to sound like an empathetic and loving, yet also broken and boring, record. For me, having verbiage written down ahead of time was helpful. The *Love and Logic* books have some great ideas, and you can adapt their language to your own voice.

Calmly and empathetically, I would say things like, "It's okay to be bored," "I trust you'll find something to do," or simply, "That's a bummer." And I really did care. It can be hard to muddle through not knowing what to do. I'd just put my little playlist of sayings on shuffle (or even repeat), and eventually the child would get sick of hearing the same thing over and over again . . . and go find something to do.

Kim John Payne gives us good direction in *The Soul of Discipline*: "You have to become really boring and leave them alone to solve the puzzle of what to do with their newfound alone time."[15]

Though this might be stressful for the parent, I was encouraged to hear Dr. Jennifer Taitz say that stress in moderation is actually a good thing. She deems it "part of the price we pay for living a life that matters."[16] What you're doing matters. By choosing to home educate, you are doing so many things that are beneficial for your children, for your family as a whole, and for yourself. It's probably going to cause a little extra (or a lot of extra) strain at times. Dunk your face in a large bowl of ice water and keep going.

When your child expresses boredom, you can use your boring, flat response to help send your child off into a state of blissful play. If that doesn't happen, provide some scaffolding. We are all learning to become. We are learning what we love. We are learning how to use open spaces of time.

You could have a simple list of ideas printed out. Post it somewhere. You could use the good ole popsicle-stick-with-ideas-written-on-them strategy or put some different ideas on small slips of paper in a jar, ready to be pulled out when needed. Sometimes we just need a jumping-off point.

Austin Kleon is one of my favorite authors who writes on getting our creativity flowing. During an interview, he told me about Art Spiegelman, an American cartoonist and editor who had different workstations for different projects. That spurred Austin to create an "analog desk." At his analog desk, nothing electronic is allowed. Many homes wouldn't have the space for more than one desk (if there's a desk at all), so an alternative idea is to have certain areas of your home where nothing digital is allowed. When you go to your analog desk or other non-digital space, "there's nothing to do unless you do it. It's a way to trick your brain to do stuff," Austin says.[17]

Going outside without electronics provides similar promptings. We're on our own.

My list of free-time ideas that I printed out when our kids were younger included the following: puppets, Play-Doh, clay, fort building, Mad Libs, finger knitting, drawing, coloring, LEGOs, story writing, comic creating, sensory bin, dollhouse, wool needle felting, reading, MAGNA-TILES, blocks, origami, watercolor painting, piano, stamps, stencil, magnets, bead crafts, baking, Perler Beads, paper dolls, sewing, string games, soccer, bike riding, xylophone, dominoes, dancing, outdoor play, marble run, stickers, puzzles, chores, lacing toys, Spirograph, schoolwork, hula hoop, playing with siblings, tangrams, kinetic sand, jump rope, cleaning, and cooking a meal.

A list like that even makes *me* excited about life. Certainly, this isn't a comprehensive list, and yet look at how many exciting things there are to do!

I printed out a list of games as well. Our family loves the card games Skip-Bo, Five Crowns, Uno, Old Maid, War, Solitaire, Go Fish, Rummy, Spoons, and Peanut (which also goes by Nertz and many other names). We love the board games Monopoly, Clue, Life, Battleship, chess, Risk, Azul, and checkers. We also love charades, Quiz, Suspend, Hot Potato, Pictionary, Balderdash, Sneaky Squirrel, and Tenzi.

As our kids grew, so did the length of our lists.

You can incorporate these lists into something Jon Acuff calls "Turn Down Techniques."[18] Have a list of three to five go-to activities that help you dial back feelings of stress in your life. These ideas are as individual as they come. For me, sewing with a machine drives me mad—I'm constantly ripping out stitches. Running makes my teeth hurt. For others, these two activities might mean bliss. By exposing our children to various hobbies and all sorts of different ideas of things to do, we give them a lifetime of strategies to turn to during hard seasons.

As a child, I remember being bored. But I was used to it. I wasn't panicked by the feeling because I knew it would leave eventually. I had a charming little dollhouse in my closet that we had gotten secondhand and that I filled with miniatures and Calico Critters. I played with it through my middle school years. I painted the floors and walls. I rearranged furniture and came up with elaborate family scenes. This was a space I could always turn to.

## Boredom Is Healthy

In a world of optimization and best practices, our homeschool lives can seem a far cry from ideal. From an outsider's perspective, it may seem that we are using the worst practices or, truthfully, no practices at all. We are winging it because there is a lot to get done and not enough time to get it done.

I'll never forget when I read Nicholas Kardaras's book *Glow Kids* and reached the quote that kicked off this chapter: "There is nothing healthier for a child than to learn how to use their own interior resources to work through the challenges of being bored."[19]

What a statement. Nothing healthier? As a society, we are in hot pursuit of avoiding the healthiest thing for children.

Jodi Musoff, an educational specialist at the Child Mind Institute, says, "Boredom also helps children develop planning strategies, problem-solving skills, flexibility, and organizational skills—key abilities that children whose lives are usually highly structured may lack."[20]

What's also amazing is that boredom so often leads to play. Susan Linn explains the value of play when she writes, "Play comes naturally to children. They play—often without knowing they are doing so—to express themselves and to gain a sense of control over their world. But play is continually devalued and stunted. For children who are flooded continually with stimuli and commands to react, the cost is high."[21]

Susan took things a step further when she told me that "children who play creatively are not lucrative to the toy industry." She said, "Toy companies don't just market products; they market values, and the value that they're marketing is that the things we buy will make us happy."[22] Acceptance of boredom as part of an ordinary yet fulfilling life is a value we are passing on.

A study in the *Journal of Industrial Product Design Research and Studies* reminds us that it is still the simple, open-ended toys that offer kids the most benefits. "One way to stimulate children's cognitive development is through the use of open-ended toys. Open-ended toys are a type of toy that provides space for interpretation and can be used in various ways to trigger children's creativity." It was the "puzzles, building blocks, and animal figurines" that stimulated cognitive growth by "increasing children's attention span, language skills, fine motor skills, and gross motor skills."[23] No bells, whistles, or batteries needed!

On the surface, I rue our open-ended days. I would feel so much better about myself if every minute were accounted for. But our children's neurological systems know what's up. They have a say. Boredom is good. It is healthy even.

Depending on the ages and stages of your kids, this knowledge opens the door to juggling some outside work. There are many single mothers who homeschool. There are single fathers who homeschool. There are a vast number of families where both parents have their hands in some sort of income-producing work and yet still manage to home educate. This is because they realize there is value in not re-creating a nine-to-four school day filled with schedules and bells. The benefits of open-ended play extend to a parent who is juggling all the homeschool job duties listed earlier, plus a career on top of it all.

**Fear Not**

In this chapter, we have explored the multifaceted role of boredom in childhood development.

Boredom is not a condition to be feared or avoided. Instead, it is a crucial element that fosters creativity, independence, and self-discovery among children. Boredom challenges children to engage with their inner world, to invent, and to explore, thereby laying the groundwork for a lifetime of learning and innovation. We must not shield our children from boredom but instead embrace it as a powerful catalyst for growth. It is essential to resist the cultural pressure to fill every moment of a child's day with structured activities and digital distractions. Instead, we should provide spaces and opportunities for them to experience the fruitful solitude that boredom can offer.

By shifting our perspective on boredom from a sign of poor parenting to a necessary space for growth, we can enhance our children's ability to entertain themselves, solve problems, and engage with the world in meaningful ways. So the next time you see your child staring out the window or fiddling aimlessly, remember: In that moment of inactivity, a world of thought, creativity, and potential is stirring. Embrace it, encourage it, and watch as your child, and perhaps even you, flourish in ways you never anticipated.

Sometimes your homeschool days appear to float. There is no regimen. There are only open doors and open possibilities. Real life is your enrichment. All the space you're leaving for boredom (much of which may be unintentional) is one of the many things you are doing right as a homeschool family.

# You Are Providing Multi-Age Experiences

> Children learn from anything and everything they see. They learn wherever they are, not just in special learning places.
>
> —John Holt, *Learning All the Time*[1]

There are many striking differences between homeschooling and traditional schooling, but perhaps the most remarkable is the exposure to people of other ages. While Dr. Peter Gray is probably the foremost expert on the benefits of spending time with people of different ages, it just makes sense on a logical level that it is important we spend time with people of various ages and abilities because that is how life is constructed.

I love how John Taylor Gatto puts it. He pulls no punches when he writes, "It is absurd and anti-life to be part of a system that compels you to sit in confinement with people of exactly the same age and social class. That system effectively cuts you off from the immense diversity of life and the synergy of variety; indeed, it cuts you off from your own past and future, sealing you in a continuous present much the same way television does."[2]

Absurd. Anti-life.

It's at least something to pause and consider. Once you graduate from high school, and for sure from college, this segmenting by age ceases to exist. Even in nursing homes there are no separate wings for eighty-six-year-olds or eighty-seven-year-olds. We begin life segregated by age, spend the entirety of childhood this way, and then leave it for good once the school years are over. College environments can still be rather homogeneous, but people often go back to school to continue their education outside of the typical college age span, which is commendable. Homeschooled children naturally engage with people of various ages in everyday settings like family gatherings, community events, and even regular visits to parks and libraries.

When we choose to do something out of convenience, such as grouping children together by age to move them through the same set of curricula, it is important to peel back the onion a little bit. Is this approach also beneficial for the child, or is it a choice solely based on practicalities?

There are a handful of questions about homeschooling that get asked repeatedly. One of them is how to homeschool across many grade levels. We are so accustomed to this grades-based approach to education that we can't possibly conceive of juggling more than one grade at a time, let alone several grades. Some dismantling has to happen here regarding many things, such as when children should be expected to learn certain material, what material they should be expected to learn, and if the timing of it truly matters.

But the question of how to homeschool across grade levels goes far deeper than grade-specific learning expectations. What if we reframe it to focus on what we are missing when we confine children by age and other commonalities? What do they lose? What do we lose as a society as a whole?

This topic takes us to deeper places. What even is education, really? If it truly is a series of facts and information that every year is disseminated and deposited into the minds of children in an assembly-line-type fashion, then our approach makes sense. But this is a narrow view of education, childhood, and children overall.

## Children Looking Up to Other Children

As Dr. Peter Gray says, "Children are biologically designed to self-educate."[3] He says this over and over again in a myriad of ways. Is it true? Dr. Gray certainly lays out substantial and robust evidence pointing in that direction, but we can also reflect on our own personal experiences. We have seen it with our eyes and felt it in our bones. Being around other people who are different from us stretches us in ways we didn't even realize we could bend.

When others come along who have more skill or new skills, we are inspired. We strive to learn and grow. We want whatever they have on display, so we work for it. Still others come along who have less skill and are interested in us. *Who, me? You like what I do?* And we teach and train, cajole and encourage. In that process, we also learn. We experience gratitude for how far we've come. We're reminded of the growth mindset, one that says we are not fixed in skill and cognition. There are opportunities still available to us. And we gain confidence in our area of expertise because we have had to break it down for someone else.

I grew up playing the piano. It is still a great love of mine. Yearly piano recitals were a place of high anxiety (*What if I forget my notes?*) but also great hope (*Someday I might be able to play like that?*). A piano recital filled with all second graders does not evoke similar questions. When all participants are the same age, all that is bred is contempt and competition.

John Taylor Gatto has strong words about this competition. In *The Underground History of American Education*, he writes,

> The strongest meshes of the school net are invisible. Constant bidding for a stranger's attention creates a chemistry producing the common characteristics of modern schoolchildren: whining, dishonesty, malice, treachery, cruelty. Increasing competition for official favor in the dramatic fish bowl of a classroom delivers cowardly children, little people sunk in chronic boredom, little people with no apparent purpose for being alive. The full significance of the classroom as a dramatic environment, as primarily a dramatic environment, has never been properly acknowledged or examined.[4]

Even outside on the playground at school, there can be aggression. David Elkind writes about this in his book *The Power of Play*. He quotes sociologists Iona and Peter Opie in their book *Children's Games in Street and Playground*: "We have noticed that when children are herded together in the playground, which is where the educationalists and the psychologists and the social scientists gather to observe them, their play is markedly more aggressive than when they are on the street or in wild places. They indulge in duels such as 'Slappies,' 'knuckles,' and 'stinging,' in which the pleasure, if not the purpose, is to dominate the other player and to inflict pain."[5]

Unnatural environments breed undesirable behaviors.

Peter Gray writes, "The forced age segregation that occurs in school itself promotes competition and bullying and inhibits the development of nurturance. Throughout human history, children and adolescents have learned to be caring and helpful through their interactions with younger children. The age-graded school system deprives them of such opportunities."[6]

One of the beautiful parts of homeschooling is that children can spend their time with others of a variety of ages. As our years tick by, clear personality traits and interests emerge. No two children are alike. Homeschooling our kids gives them the opportunity to gravitate toward those they click with both in personality and in passion. Natural teachers who don't have advanced degrees, or any degree at all, emerge in the world and still have so much to offer.

## Increasing the Pool of Participants

I grew up at a church that segmented kids by grade level, a common practice among many churches who follow the public school approach to their children's programming. Over the years, several kids in my grade came and went, but there was only one friend who was there for the entirety of my childhood church experience. It was just the two of us.

The church split the kids' programming up by placing two grades together. The kindergartners had their own big room, but the first and second graders started Sunday school together and then broke out into smaller rooms by grade level for snack time (animal crackers and Dixie cups of lukewarm water) and a lesson. Third and fourth graders were together, and fifth and sixth graders were together. Then you were off to "big church."

I had friends in the grades immediately above and below me, but we never became all that close because each year there was a swap. You either lost the older kids and subsequently became the older kids of that class, or you moved up, leaving the younger ones behind. I thought about this a lot as a child because there were only two mainstays in my grade. If that friend was sick or out of town, I was alone. And it felt like that. The upheaval from year to year, though it may not seem like a big deal, kept kids from really connecting with those who were one grade higher or one grade lower.

When I look at our own children, at this moment and truly for most of their childhoods, each of their closest friends is not in the same exact grade. In some cases, the difference is more than one grade level.

When we siphon kids off with these arbitrary grade cutoffs, the question is not only what they are missing out on but *who* they are missing out on. There may be that special friend who just gets them, makes them laugh, and gives their world so much more meaning, but if that friend is a grade away, it might as well be a different planet. There isn't a path for connection.

In the neighborhoods of old, dozens of kids roaming the area shattered those age barriers. You played with who you could find, who you could keep up with, and who your soul connected with. The same is true for homeschooling. The diversity of family makeups creates situations where you cannot orchestrate relationships that are solely based on grade level.

You may have three families who get together, with kids who range in age from newborn to nineteen. There are all sorts of overlaps. It's possible that not a single child is in the same grade as another. And often, children in homeschool communities end up linking arms with others they never would've even passed in the hallway of a public school. As social interactions wane due to less play and more screens, it is all the more important that the pool of playmate participants be ever widening.

As a general trend, family size is decreasing. This encompasses both immediate family and extended family, affecting how many playmates are available for all kids. An article titled "Families Are Shrinking: Study Reveals Shocking Decline in Number of Relatives" by the Max Planck Society gives these shocking statistics: "The number of relatives that an individual has is expected to decrease by more than 35 percent in the near future. . . . In 1950, a 65-year-old woman had an average of 41 living relatives. By 2095, a woman of the same age will have an average of only 25 living relatives."[7] This is a global phenomenon.

Diego Alburez-Gutierrez, a researcher at the Max Planck Institute, reports, "We expect the overall size of families to decline permanently in all regions of the world." He also writes of declining "kinship resources" worldwide.[8]

As an adult, I have one dear friend who is a birthday buddy. We were born two days apart. It's special. But she is the only one close to my age. The age range of those dearest to me spans decades.

Homeschooling allows children to gain practice finding "their people." It's like the flight attendants say on an airplane: "Keep in mind that the nearest exit may be behind you." Your closest friend may be in a grade below or above you. Your closest friend may not even be born yet or may be a decade or more older than you.

Our boys play in a homeschool basketball league that operates similarly to my childhood church. Each year their teammates are switching up. Some of the teams are rather small to begin with—only five or six players. While this is common, and team sports provide certain benefits and relationships, it's even better when families come together and there are children of all ages to spend time with.

An added benefit is that, in time, your children will often get to know and enjoy their siblings' friends. Our kids remark on this often. It's a gift to befriend those your siblings enjoy and love. It helps everyone to be knit together more tightly.

## Learning Empathy Through Babies and Toddlers

Dr. Michele Borba is sounding the alarm about decreasing levels of empathy among today's kids. Developing empathy isn't something I thought much about until I read Michele's book *UnSelfie* and had a chance to talk with her about it. "Empathy is dropping while, at the same time, narcissism is rising," she told me.[9] That's not a great combination.

We are not born empathetic to the plights of others. This is something we must learn with time, and in an age of selfies and personally curated content online, we are losing the ability to put ourselves in the shoes of others. This matters because "kids who are able to read nonverbal cues are better adjusted emotionally, more popular, more outgoing, and more sensitive in general."[10]

Michele writes about a program called Roots of Empathy[11] that employs babies. The babies aren't employees in a strict sense, but they are brought into classroom settings to help children learn how to read the cues of others. Roots of Empathy was designed in 1996 by a woman named Mary Gordon, who is a bestselling author, parenting expert, Canadian educator, and social entrepreneur.

Volunteer families who have a baby between two and four months at the beginning of a school year are matched with neighborhood schools. Over the course of that school year, the baby will visit the classroom with a parent on nine separate occasions. The students observe the baby's behaviors and reactions for a time period, discuss what they are seeing with classmates and their teacher, and in doing so begin to develop empathy, as the name of the organization suggests. The Roots of Empathy website is filled with testimonials from students, teachers, and volunteer families touting the success of this program. One story that Michele recounts in *UnSelfie* stood out to me. She wrote about how the presence of the baby so moved one of the students that, as he was rocking the baby after their circle time in class together, he asked, "If nobody has ever loved you, do you think you could still be a good father?"[12]

The prevailing view is that juggling babies and toddlers amid a day of homeschooling is difficult, undesirable even. Everything would be so much better if each homeschool family had one set of quintuplets and got on with it. Each year, you would need only one set of resources. You wouldn't have to deal with varying sleep schedules or being up part of the night with a clingy toddler and then another part of the night with a concerned teen.

And yet, this Roots of Empathy program reveals that babies are in hot demand. It's more than likely that you have some in your homeschool community—or even right in your home.

If you are drowning with small kids at home, search for a homeschool community that has some eight-, eleven-, or fifteen-year-olds. Not every older child will be keen on playing with little ones, but some will. Some will flourish in it. Some will be on the edge of their seats waiting to hold your baby or to run around with a toddler.

We joined a Family Wellness Center in our community that welcomes all ages. Each one of our family members has what we call "gym friends." Our youngest child, who is currently seven, is a popular attendant in the children's class. How could a seven-year-old hold so much value? She helps with the babies! She knows their names, she makes faces at them, and she loves when they interact with her. She is truly a valuable asset to the teachers in this mixed-age playroom that allows babies through age twelve. Through these experiences, our child has the opportunity to learn what babies are like and how they develop. She has observed first wobbly steps, first words, tears, and joys. This is the "synergy of variety" that John Taylor Gatto speaks of.

## Historical Origins of Age Segregation

Sometimes we just want to close our eyes. We want to bury our heads in the sand. Parenting is hard enough, and the decisions we make about schooling have ramifications, both short-term and long-term. We already outsource a lot of life; it's tempting to outsource this decision as well. That yellow school bus arrives faithfully, rain or shine. We watch all the other neighborhood kids trudge out there day in and day out. No one would bat an eye if your family joined the routine. But you're here. You're reading this. With a desire for understanding and wisdom, you're looking intently at the world we live in. Let's examine how we ended up with the system that surrounds us and seems perfectly normal.

The modern school system we currently employ in the United States, where children are classified by age and marched along a predetermined set of learning objectives from age five through age eighteen, finds many of its roots in Prussia. Prussia was a military state that united with the German empire in 1871. It was Prussian philosophy that kicked off much of what we see today, from age grouping to the bells that ring between classes.

It all began with Frederick the Great, who was, at least in part, salty about some prior military losses. The methods set before us did not begin with grandmothers or mothers who loved their children and found unequivocally that children bound within four walls, sitting next to peers, was a lovely way to learn. No, it was Frederick the Great of Prussia who had an aim that was state-focused rather than child-focused in nature. He wanted a systematic way to create loyal citizens who were obedient. John Taylor Gatto clarified these aims in his article "Our Prussian School System":

Modern forced schooling started in Prussia in 1819 with a clear vision of what centralized schools could deliver:

1. Obedient soldiers for the army,
2. Obedient workers for the mines,
3. Subservient civil servants for government,
4. Subservient clerks for industry, and
5. Citizens who thought alike about major issues.[13]

At the heart of the Prussian influence was a philosophy of shaping the minds of children through the educational system. Teacher training and standardization of education, including standardized tests, got their start in this era. Simplification and the breaking down of education into bite-sized pieces began around this time. The Prussian model had a large focus on both structure and obedience. It was Prussia that introduced this highly organized, state-controlled education system to the rest of the world. Once new and novel, this approach that we still largely follow several hundred years later is now commonplace.

The schoolroom was largely modeled after the workplace, which is clear to see even to this day. Children go to school much like their parents go to work on a Monday-to-Friday, nine-to-five-type schedule. Kids even bring work home with them, much like their parents do these days. The school day and subsequent homework take up a vast swath of childhood that could be given to more individualized pursuits.

What we see in today's educational system was not ushered in by loving family members who cared for the children around them. Instead, it was introduced by American political leaders, industrialists, clergy, and educators, some of whom actually went to Prussia to study its methods and

100

then began bringing their findings back to the United States. Gatto explains it this way: "American ideological leaders . . . fell in love with the order, obedience, and efficiency of [the Prussian] educational system."[14]

In other words, if something has always seemed a little off to you about our approach to childhood education, that's because it is. The origins of our educational system aren't rooted in views like those of educational philosopher Charlotte Mason, who touted that "children are born persons."[15]

Mason wrote many things that are directly opposite of the Prussian views. Today, mothers around the world echo many of her sentiments, such as, "The question is not— 'how much does the youth know?' when he has finished his education—but how much does he care? And about how many orders of things does he care? In fact, how large is the room in which he finds his feet set? And, therefore, how full is the life he has before him?"[16] She adds, "Self-education is the only possible education; the rest is mere veneer laid on the surface of a child's nature."[17]

Indeed, our collective approach to education currently does not reflect the ideas of Charlotte Mason. Rather, schooling today has very similar vibes to the original Prussian system, but now it has also become big business, with contracts, careers, and prestige at stake as well. This is not to say that a child will not be able to leave a system with Prussian footprints and become successful. It is merely an opportunity to examine, and examine deeply, why we are doing what we are doing with our nation's children—and our own.

We can also glean wisdom that is passed down from generation to generation. I love what Nicholas Kardaras wrote about his father in *Digital Madness*: "He didn't understand a world dependent on technology—one where people didn't look each other in the eye, where they were stuck in front of screens for hours on end and felt lost and empty. He hates what he sees as our tech obsessions." Nicholas's father would say things like, "Stop looking at that stupid thing and be *here* if you're going to be here."[18]

Dr. John Delony wrote about his grandmother in his book *Building a Non-Anxious Life*: "For many years my grandmother had been telling me to turn off the television (or video games) and go outside. To play with my friends (or play dominoes with her). To walk or ride my bike instead of drive." She also advised him "to stop eating junk. To have adventures. To read and exercise. To play a musical instrument. To pray and be part of a faith community."[19]

Not only did she give directives, but she modeled this lifestyle. John says, "She's been telling me and showing me."[20]

Everything John's grandmother suggested is now thoroughly backed by science.

*Bike instead of drive:* Biomechanist Katy Bowman told me that "our bodies are built for a tremendous amount of movement" as we discussed her book *Rethink Your Position.*[21] She added, "So much of our environment is beckoning us to sit and scroll."[22] Dan Buettner, a top researcher on centenarians, echoed Katy when he told me, "Physical activity is absolutely necessary for healthy aging. Fewer than 25% of Americans get the absolute minimum."[23]

*Go outside:* You will find evidence of this in a multitude of places, but Dr. Victoria Dunckley summarized it well in her book *Reset Your Child's Brain*: "What do children require to develop optimally? Kids need several hours of unstructured physical play daily to adequately stimulate and integrate sensory pathways; they need secure attachment to caregivers, plenty of touch, and varying levels of environmental stimulation that support calm alertness during the day and restful sleep at night. They also need conversation with adults, contact with nature, and creative outlets, such as music, art or dance."[24]

*Turn off the television:* Jonathan Haidt recently wrote a bestselling book called *The Anxious Generation.*[25] When we discussed portions of it, he echoed this advice. "TV is not particularly harmful," he said, but "it blocks out other activities."[26]

We could so easily find studies these days to back all the other advice from John Delony's grandmother. But when she was doling out advice to her grandson, she didn't have the studies about what researchers have spent decades trying to determine. So I asked John, "How did she know?"

He told me that all grandparents knew because this was how people lived for "all of human history until like forty years ago. They went through everything and they really lined it up. Here's how you live: Go outside, have friends, be with people. Eat in moderation, laugh until it hurts. If you're going to have a drink, don't do it every day. But when you do, make sure you've got people with you so y'all can be extra silly, right?"

John went on to tell a poignant story about food. "I remember so distinctly. It was an interview with a group of grandmothers. It was about margarine. And they had grown up on these farms and made their own butter for years. I remember this group of grandmothers saying, 'We knew this was wrong. We looked at this bucket of margarine, and we knew it wasn't healthy, but they kept telling us that the experts said we were hurting our kids by giving them butter. And so we made the switch to this tub of chemicals.' And now, of course, I don't know anybody that has margarine anymore, but it's been this shift, but these grandmothers knew."

John talks about the irony of growing up hearing all sorts of hilarious stories about his grandparents and chickens, but then they eventually moved from an area with amazing wildlife to "a very, very small two-bedroom house in a suburb of Houston right by the highway." John's grandmother, who had grown up "on a chicken farm in the middle of hot Texas," eventually was serving Grape Nuts and Spam.[27]

Sometimes we lose our way. Sometimes we fall apart. Sometimes we forget to take the perspective of someone who has shown up here for the first time—perhaps a stranger from a far-off land. Would a newcomer look at this age-segregation strategy and the way we quarantine children based on grade levels and conclude that it's the ideal choice? Does it truly make sense for your child to be educated based on Prussian ideals from the 1800s?

Dr. Peter Gray explains our entrenchment this way: "School is the most predominant cultural ritual of our time. It is a practice ingrained as normal, even necessary, in the minds of the great majority of people. To counter it, one must overcome not just others' negative judgments but also the judgments that rise up from one's own school-indoctrinated mind."[28]

Steven Pressfield writes in *The War of Art*, "Our job in this lifetime is not to shape ourselves into some ideal we imagine we ought to be, but to find out who we already are and become it."[29]

## The Case for Less Age-Specific Instruction

One fear of moving away from an age-specific model of instruction is that there will be less individual instruction overall throughout the course of a childhood, and this stands to be true. Most likely, it is not possible for a mother with three children of differing ages, for example, to provide grade-specific lessons for each child throughout all thirteen years of schooling. Or at least it isn't as straightforward as it might be in a classroom setting.

Yet Dr. Peter Gray talks about an eye-opening experiment in New Hampshire showing that "children who were taught less learned more."[30] He introduces L. P. Benezet, who was the superintendent of schools in Manchester, New Hampshire, in the late 1920s and early 1930s. "Benezet showed that kids who received just one year of arithmetic, in sixth grade, performed at least as well on standard calculations and much better on story problems, than kids who had received several previous years of arithmetic training." Dr. Gray goes on to question, "Why have almost no educators heard of this experiment? Why isn't Benezet now considered to be one of the geniuses of public education? I wonder."[31]

How encouraging that a loosening of the reins could lead to more success. Your chaotic home filled with children of varying ages, interests, skill sets, and passions might lead to better outcomes solely because you can't quite keep up with them all; they are being taught less and yet learning more. What appears to be a negative turns out to be a positive!

I certainly had some moments before I began to learn about the benefits of multi-age experiments when I wished I had given birth to multiples. *I should've eaten more yams*, I thought. But then I learned that what has been touted as the ideal—dividing kids off by age and sequestering them into groups for their entire childhood—wasn't invented for the sake of the child. So pat yourself on the back, homeschool parent. By simply keeping your child home, you are exposing them to multi-age environments on a regular basis, whether that is with siblings, other family members, your homeschool community, or beyond.

As an added bonus, providing multi-age experiences enriches everyone involved. Younger children learn from the older ones, absorbing skills and knowledge beyond their years, while older children gain patience, leadership, and a sense of responsibility. These interactions mimic real-life social settings, preparing kids for a world where people of all ages and backgrounds work and grow together. When you choose to homeschool, you're already creating an environment that mirrors the collaborative nature of life outside the school walls, equipping your children with skills they will use for a lifetime. There are so many things you are already doing right, simply by choosing to home educate.

# You Are Modeling

Adults must use the skills they have where children can see them. . . . Children need to get some sense of the processes by which good work is done.

— John Holt, *Learning All the Time*[1]

Occasionally, I read things I wish I hadn't. I wish I could go back in time just a few seconds, erase a passage I'd just read out of my brain, set the book down, and never pick it up again.

The passage above from John Holt is an example of something I wanted to immediately delete because it challenged me. I read it when our oldest was around eight years old with four younger siblings. Though we had already delayed our foray into formal education, I still held a tight grip on some of the pieces that gave me a semblance of control.

But then I read that passage in this context:

This isn't a matter of "giving" harder tasks and making the child persist until he or she is finished. . . . Instead, what young children need is the opportunity to see older children

107

and adults choosing and undertaking various tasks and working on them over a period of time until they are completed. Children need to get some sense of the processes by which good work is done. The only way they can learn how much time and effort it takes to build, say, a table, is to be able to see someone building a table, from start to finish. Or painting a picture. Or repairing a bicycle, or writing a story, or whatever it may be.[2]

Ugh.

This was a different level of commitment. I was convicted.

Homeschooling involves not just directing the learning but living out the learning process in a way I hadn't anticipated. And yet, it is possible that a kid could live an entire childhood and not have any sense of how good work is carried out and completed. So often, kids are not a part of the decision-making process. They are simply told to do this or that and then they comply (or sometimes they don't).

Here I was, going full speed ahead in one direction, but now I knew I had to make some changes. I could not read a passage like that and continue on as the orchestrator of all the homeschool details.

At first, I tried to outsource this responsibility. My husband, Josh, traveled for work. He gave presentations around the country.

"Any chance you could take the kids?" I asked him.

"No. Not a chance," he responded.

"Any chance you could set up a phone or an iPad before you speak and sort of, I don't know, like livestream it so we can watch from home?" I pressed on.

"Absolutely not" was the final answer.

Pointing out that he was defying these thought-provoking words of John Holt did nothing to move the needle. Tacking ourselves onto Dad's work wasn't an option.

The problem was, I didn't have much to offer. At that time, I felt overwhelmed and underprepared, struggling to keep up with even basic tasks. I wasn't designing cupcakes that looked like flowers or making cookies with frosting that depicted a snow globe. I wasn't selling roadside cut flowers or mixing essential oil potions. It felt like such a tremendous task to model adult processes, and I didn't want the added pressure of figuring this out. And yet, it felt imperative.

John Holt went on. Of course he did. A few paragraphs later, I got an extra nudge.

> Adults must use the skills they have where children can see them. In the unlikely event that they have no skills to speak of, they should learn some, and let the children see them learning, even if only as simple a thing as touch typing. They should invite children to join them in using these skills. In this way children can be slowly drawn, at higher and higher levels of energy, commitment, and skill, into more and more serious and worthwhile adult activities.[3]

Holt didn't let anyone off the hook. My lack of skills didn't give me a free pass. No, instead I was commissioned to learn something and let our kids watch. No one likes to display their learning, and yet here I was, holding a book in my hand that would end up changing the trajectory of our family. I just didn't know it yet.

### "Adults Must"

"Must" is such strong language. I knew I couldn't skirt around this one. As I was still mulling over my lack of skills, an opportunity presented itself. And I was annoyed about it. The words of John Holt compelled me to say yes. So this is the story of how I became both an author and a photographer in a period of three months, when I was neither of those things before.

A publisher reached out to me about writing a book. And it wasn't an algebra book. It was a *book* book. One with paragraphs and words. Immediately I was out of my element. Some love to write. I'm preferential to equations. Growing up, I never even reread my first drafts at school. Some people don't like to listen to the sound of their own voice. This was the case for me with writing. If I read a piece of writing back to myself, I might be embarrassed at what had sprung forth from within me. My whole body cringed. I wasn't a second-draft type of person.

This outlook didn't bode well for becoming an author. But remember, I didn't really want to become an author in the first place. I was trying to model lifelong growth and learning. I was trying to give our kids a front-row seat to a process that I knew nothing about and wasn't remotely confident in.

Reluctantly, I said yes. And then I proceeded to tell the editor that it had always been in my heart to write a book called *Until the Streetlights Come On*, about how a return to play during childhood enhances all our lives while also preparing our kids for what they will need in the future.

Little did I know that all publishing companies are different. Often they specialize in different types of books. And this company hadn't reached out to hear my idea. They had their own idea. They wanted me to write an outdoor activity book—but I'm not good at crafts. I was also supposed to be the photographer, and I didn't know how to do that. And the manuscript was due in three months—might I add, for very little pay.

Clearly the answer was no, but that darn John Holt passage . . .

Adults must.

## Learning in Public

So I said yes and set out to learn how to become a professional photographer, a professional writer, and a professional crafter in the span of one-fourth of one year (I had to throw the math in there). This was a steep learning curve for me. I researched basic photography online, took two online courses, and then tried to practice daily if at all possible. I joined online forums and sent in questions. I never nail things on the first try, and often not on the second either. I don't naturally have an eye for setups and layouts and background scenes. As I stumbled through the basics of photography, I involved our kids by asking for their opinions on photos and letting them suggest different layouts for my next shoot. This not only helped me view my work from different perspectives but also involved my children in the learning process.

Reflect on a time when you learned something new in front of your children. What was their reaction? What do you think they learned from observing you?

Slowly but surely, one step at a time, my children and I worked our way through this book project. We clipped our nails (a publisher requirement) and changed into clothes without branding (an additional requirement). We played with all sorts of natural elements and made fairies out of pine cones, dollhouses out of pumpkins, and games out of acorn caps. It was delightful. I was reminded of the power of simplicity.

We invited friends and family to join in. The crafts and activities took shape and fit into enticing chapter categories like forest dwellers, garden tinkers, outdoor artists, and puddle stompers. I snapped photo after photo, adjusting ISO and aperture—words I wouldn't have known just a few weeks prior. I learned how to edit photos and what a TIFF file was.

By December 2020, I had completed the manuscript and sent it off. Finished. Complete. My editor's encouraging response soon followed.

"Congratulations, Ginny! You should feel very proud of putting together such a fine manuscript so efficiently. One of the best, in my experience."

Tears fall now as I type that out. I had no idea what I was doing. I confronted several skill sets where I had not one skill. I saw the reward. My kids saw the reward. It was so much more than just the book.

## Challenges and Triumphs

Next on the agenda was learning the marketing side of things. I was excited and anxious to step into yet another new realm. At each point where my nerves threatened loudly to take over, I went back to John Holt. Modeling is something I had to do, at least in some measure, for the sake of our kids. This meant showing them how to take risks. My learning process reminded me of their learning plights, each of ours on different scales but no less intimidating for the individual.

In January of 2021, the company sent a BLAD (book layout and design). One step in a new direction led to acquiring gobs of new knowledge. I remember where I was when I first saw the BLAD. I was sitting in the driveway at a friend's house on a snowy January day. This friend happened to have an indoor pool (score!), and we were headed inside to make some memories. But first, I glanced through the sample layout. And I was shocked at how beautiful it was.

I had delivered words and pictures, and they turned it into a book. An actual, real-life book. The BLAD contained just a small section of the book, but it looked phenomenal. It was beyond what I could have imagined. I typed out a quick reply and gathered up our swimming stuff to try to make it through another blustery day in Michigan.

> I am head over heels for this. I can't even describe how much I love it. I even cried. I also cried after your last email which was so encouraging!!
>
> This is beyond thrilling. I love how colorful it is and I love all the extra cheery elements that were added in. It think it fits the audience perfectly and I couldn't be happier with it!

Perhaps you caught the typo in the last sentence. That is really what I sent off. To a book editor. "It think."

Interestingly, I learned that even though grammar and catching typos aren't my strong suit, there are other people in the world who take care of that part. Who love that part, even. Go figure.

As I shed tears in the driveway, I had a fuller picture of what John Holt was advocating for, and indeed, this stepping into a new skill enriched the lives of our family in ways I couldn't have anticipated.

## The Day After the BLAD

The day after the BLAD came through, while I was still walking on clouds and shooting off screenshots of the pre-finished project to all our friends and family, my editor asked if I could have a phone call. Sure! I envisioned celebrations and cheering. Maybe there would be a party going on in the background while we discussed how this book could reach the ends of the earth. Maybe others were clamoring for translated copies. Maybe there would be a bonus for my "efficient" manuscript.

It was the end of the day Friday when the call came through, and I had it on speakerphone so anyone within earshot could share in the triumph of my first John Holt accomplishment. I had learned not just one thing but many new things. Right in front of our kids. They got to see a project go from the starting line to the finish line. They would enter their teen and adult years with a better sense of the time and effort required to write a book. When they hit their own roadblocks in life, I could remind them of a time when I, too, was stuck but bravely moved forward and reaped the rewards.

The phone call went in a different direction.

"Due to COVID," my editor said, "our budget has been restructured. We are having to cut many books that were set to launch in 2021, and I regret to inform you that your book will not be published."

Just like that, it was over.

I was not only embarrassed but confused. Less than twenty-four hours after reaching out to my friends and family, I had to walk back my exuberant texts showing this wonderful BLAD and instead inform everyone that the book was no more.

That's when the questions started piling up in my body. *What are you doing with your life? Why did you say yes in the first place? You knew you weren't cut out for that level of work. Are you sure you know what you're doing with this homeschooling thing? Because you sure botched this.* Worse than the humiliation was the questioning. I lost my footing.

I thought this was what I was supposed to do.

And then our brains started to spin—Josh's and mine.

This book was done. Completely finished. All it needed was a designer, and lo and behold, we knew of a good one. A good friend of ours, a homeschool dad we had known for years—long before we even had kids—had done the layout for many books, including some of his own. So we called up our buddy and the owner and founder of Saint Creative, Carl Johnson, and asked if he would take on our project. He enthusiastically said yes and nailed it. We were even able to add testimonials that came in from around the world. Once the book became fully ours, we were able to take it in the direction we wanted it to go.

Annie from Florida wrote in and said, "My family has been saved by 1000 Hours Outside! As a former early-childhood educator, I was confident with homeschooling my two toddlers. I was not, however, prepared for the hardships that came with a global pandemic and social isolation. Finding a supportive group of parents with an endless supply of inspiration and creative outdoor ideas has been an amazing blessing. Our own backyard is now our favorite place to be!"

Barbara from Michigan sent this: "Hi Ginny! I just wanted to say thank you for all the work you do. I never knew what an impact your mission would have on me. After a miscarriage in 2019, your challenge pulled me out of the deep sadness and grief I was feeling. Being intentional about spending outside time with my 3 boys changed my soul as well as my kids. It seems like such a small thing, but in fact has impacted me in more ways than you know. We finished our first year of intentional outside time, and we are changed. We just had our sweet rainbow baby, and she is already racking up hours outside. Thank you."

Words poured in from families far and wide.

A book that had died was quickly brought back to life. Now we just needed to handle the rest of the marketing process on our own, with no skills or knowledge of how to do it.

We bought our own run of books with the intent to sell them through our website. We had been in the e-commerce space for less than a year and up until that point sold only T-shirts and stickers. There was a lot to sort through in terms of packaging and shipping, as well as the looming question of how many (if any) books would sell.

## Everyday Modeling at Home

When I was under contract with the publisher, they had set the initial publication date of the *1000 Hours Outside Activity Book* for November of 2021. Once an author turns in a manuscript, it is often about a year before the final book actually makes it into a customer's hand. One of the reasons it takes this long is because sometimes the large run of books is printed overseas, and they simply take a while to get where they need to be.

But our self-published books were printed right here in the United States, so we were able to get them quickly.

The pallets arrived on April 29, 2021, and on April 30, by complete happenstance, I was featured on *The Today Show* with Dylan Dreyer.

Our books sold out.

You are holding in your hand my eighth book. Eighth. From a person who never wrote a second draft in her entire K–12 education. You are reading words that are a product of my own homeschooling and learning as an adult, when I thought all my schooling was already behind me.

The lessons our family has carried forth from this singular "yes" to a challenge posed by a man who passed away when I was just four years old are unparalleled. And we never could have imagined the doors that have opened for our entire family because of this "yes."

What I've learned over the years is that we are modeling simply by choosing to have our children around us. It doesn't take writing a book or having a side hustle to give our kids a deeper glimpse into the adult world. Children who are around a nurturing family for the majority of their childhood begin to learn how to craft a life.

They learn how to take care of others. They learn how to make shifts when things aren't going well. They learn how to rest during hard seasons. They learn how to plan meals and grocery shop. They learn what to say to a hurting friend. They learn how to deal with feelings of inadequacy. They learn how to find answers to the questions they have. They learn how to budget. They learn how to plan a trip. They learn from you and about you. They learn the beautiful craft of family building. They learn the value of hard work and sacrifice. They learn how to find enjoyment in life. They learn how to jump for joy and how to cry tears that fill a bucket. They learn how to sort through personality conflicts. They learn how to fall and pick themselves back up again.

In your home, modeling some of these behaviors may look like planning a small home improvement project and involving children in each step, from planning to execution. Or it might look like cooking a new recipe together, as you explain the process and the importance of each ingredient. Earlier this year, we did a bedroom switch-around for our oldest daughter, and she was involved in every step, from choosing the paint color to applying the paint to arranging her bedroom furniture and wall decor. Small opportunities like this that will arise throughout childhood will teach kids about planning, preparation, and the satisfaction of seeing a project through to completion.

Adelaide Olguin, founder of Talkbox.Mom, has a program that teaches the whole family how to talk in a foreign language, and she is also passionate about international travel. She told me in a podcast interview that she allows her children to help plan their family trips.[4] The family begins with a vision for their trip that often involves literature, history, science, art, music, or their family history. Then they incorporate skills like managing a budget, and they help choose the dates because she doesn't want anybody "whining that it was somebody's birthday party."

"Who doesn't want their kids to be able to write, save for a goal, manage an itinerary, research options and make recommendations, compare prices, and pitch ideas?" Adelaide asks.

There are always constraints in life. No family can execute every single idea in one trip. Each sibling has unique ideas and interests. Being involved in the planning helps the kids learn how to pitch their own ideas in a way that gets them buy-in from others. For example, they might hope to convince their family to go to the Pokémon Café in Japan and eat the Pokémon pancakes.

Throughout their travels, the Olguins use journals to enhance their learning. Author and world-renowned nature journaler John Muir Laws advocates for journaling, reminding us that journals help us "see, remember, and stimulate curiosity."[5] The Olguins' travel journals are a place where Adelaide's kids can write down the questions they form about their travels, leading to academic research—even for her young children.

Finally, Adelaide's kids present their research to immediate and extended family in a myriad of ways. They combine photography, videography, writing, photo and video editing, and graphic design in their presentations. They include interview questions they've asked people they met along their journey. They combine all of this with Microsoft Word, PowerPoint, Canva, InDesign, Illustrator, and Adobe Premiere Pro.

Adelaide told me about their two-year-old's research journal. When their family visited Chichén Itzá, he was fascinated by the stairs, as any toddler would be. But these stairs in particular are fascinating to anyone. The parents and kids counted the stairs as they went up them, and then they took pictures to put in the two-year-old's research journal since he was too young to write anything on his own.

Over the years, he would look back through his journal, and as he got older, the entire family would talk about how each of the sides of the pyramid had a staircase with ninety-one steps. All four stairways of ninety-one steps plus one extra step at the top add up to 365, the number of days in a year. And there's more! At each equinox, the afternoon sun will hit the northern staircase just right so that it looks like a snake is creeping down the stairs.

Fast-forward two and half years. After lots of looking back through the pictures in his journal and talking about them, Adelaide's then four-and-a-half-year-old son walked up to an archaeologist at the Perot Museum of Nature and Science in Dallas and correctly identified a little statue the archaeologist was holding as Chichén Itzá. Then the little boy began spouting off all these facts he knew, like the ninety-one stairs on each side. Adelaide told me that the two of them were having such a deep conversation that she had to break them up after twenty minutes to go on to other things.

Life is inherently interesting. When we step back and take a wide view, there is so much we can learn. It would be easy to take the lead, promoting what catches our attention as parents, but Adelaide says, "It's not the question the parent is interested in; it's the question the child is interested in."[6] Adelaide has modeled and structured the type of life that leads to asking questions. The project management and research skills that her kids gain through planning their travels are unparalleled.

Involve your children in anything you can. Can they go over the weekly grocery list and budget with you? Can they be involved in the meal planning? Can they help with making small purchasing decisions? Can they help with the vacation planning? In a typical day at home, identify two or three activities in which you could more actively involve your children, allowing them to learn by watching and participating.

What are three or four different skills you possess that you could demonstrate and teach to your children? How could you weave these skills into your life on a more regular basis? Look for areas that would enhance your own personal growth, knowing that if you learn in front of your children, it's a valuable opportunity for them to learn as well. And then consider reversing the roles. Let your child teach you something that they do well or are passionate about.

Michaeleen Doucleff writes in *Hunt, Gather, Parent* that "children don't see a difference between adult work and play. Real-life events are the 'enrichment activities.'"[7] Even things as mundane as choosing a watermelon at the grocery store or vacuuming your living room can be both entertaining and "tools for learning and growing, physically and emotionally"[8] for your children.

Instead of viewing ourselves as entertainers, let's just be who we are. Being present is enough.

My midwife and dear friend Beth S. Barbeau, founder of Indigo Forest, told me about an author, midwife, and Waldorf teacher named Rahima Baldwin, who wrote the book *You Are Your Child's First Teacher*. Baldwin observed, "The imitative nature of the baby and young child is so obvious and so all-pervasive that we tend to be blind to it, unaware of its implications for parenting. . . . Your child learns everything through imitation—walking, talking, toilet training, tying shoes, endless tasks. And imitation manifests in expressions and gestures, as when we see and hear ourselves in our children's play."[9]

This shouldn't stop once a child reaches school age. Yet, as a society, we press the pause button on intentionally modeling behaviors for our children for the good part of thirteen years, shuffle kids wearing a robe and a hat with a tassel across a stage, place a rolled-up diploma in their hands, and tell them to get at it. But get at what? They haven't been exposed to much beyond all that they've been instructed to do by others.

This is how we end up with college students who, as Professor Jean Twenge told me, "can't even make simple decisions without texting their parents."[10]

On the other end of the spectrum, you have a child like Joelle Hanscom, who is just wrapping up her senior year after spending the vast majority of her childhood playing in the woods. Her mother, Angela, is the founder of the TimberNook program and the author of a personal favorite book of mine, *Balanced and Barefoot*. Joelle didn't have a cell phone until the ninth grade, and she attributes relational skills to a self-directed childhood, saying, "I can hold a conversation with a person that lasts longer than a minute." She noticed that "while most kids my age struggle with their identities, I know exactly who I am" and that "people appreciate when you're yourself." Joelle challenges all of us by saying, "A childhood on the screens is not really a childhood."[11]

As you take up this job of parenting 24/7, you are also teaching your child how to parent. Author and speaker Heidi St. John tells moms, "Don't misunderstand the value of what you're doing." At the tail end of her active mothering years, Heidi realized, "All this time I was raising parents for my grandchildren."[12]

## Executive Functioning

John Holt didn't use this terminology, but seeing a project through to the end is a part of what's referred to as executive functioning. Dr. Victoria Dunckley explains, "Attention is a component of executive functioning," and essentially, "executive functioning is getting things done."[13]

Michele Borba adds in *UnSelfie*: "A University of Colorado study found that kids who spent too much time in structured extra activities, like academics and sports, were *less* able to use their executive function skills (a broad range of crucial thinking skills like planning, problem-solving, and decision making) than children who spent *more* time engaged in free play. In fact, the *more* time kids spend in structured activities, the *less* able they were to use executive function."[14]

Developmental psychologist Dr. Aliza Pressman has nearly two decades of experience working with families, and she told me, "Pretend play is the best way to bolster executive function."[15]

When you are homeschooling, kids are exposed to years and years of natural sequences that play out from start to end and aren't interrupted by the ringing of bells. Homeschooling allows children to experience projects and follow deep dives into learning from start to finish, uninterrupted by the structured schedules of traditional schooling.

I often write in our bedroom because our office chair is exceedingly uncomfortable. From where I sit (in our bed), I can see our backyard and watch the chickens run around. They've got a good thing going out there. They run as a pack, snagging bugs along the way.

Mid-paragraph, I noticed one of our favorites, Hey-Hey, a small but mighty bantam rooster, hobbling around. Something was wrong. I watched as Josh and a few of our kids went out to investigate. They made several attempts to corner Hey-Hey. I could imagine the conversation even though I couldn't hear it.

"You go this way."

"You go that way."

"Can someone shut the gate?"

"If we corner him over there, I'll be able to pick him up."

Eventually, the dream team was holding the chicken, freeing him from some string that had basically wound both of his legs together. This is executive functioning, and it's a different breed from the type of accomplishment that involves finishing a workbook or reading an entire textbook.

Maybe all of this should help us celebrate more. Any time you finish anything, you've modeled executive functioning. You got a meal on the table? You got *three* meals on the table in one day? You got the diapers changed? A floor swept? Some stories read? A rooster freed from the tangles of a string? Let's hear it for the executive functioning skills that you are modeling day in and day out for your children as they follow you around everywhere. It's all out in the open. Kids get to see the behind-the-scenes stuff, and they want to see the behind-the-scenes stuff. We all do.

## The Ripple Effect

Self-publishing a book was actually part two of a series of events spurred on by the charge to model more and direct less. Part one involved a one-thousand-dollar investment in a line of 1000 Hours Outside T-shirts, which ended up paving the way for part two.

We landed on the idea of launching a small line of branded T-shirts as a family so we could allow our kids to be part of a very small business. A man at our church was in the T-shirt business. He came to our house for our first business meeting. Everyone joined in. Each child, even the ones who couldn't write yet, sat around our kitchen table with a piece of paper and something to write (or scribble) with. We negotiated colors and designs and landed on our final product together.

We walked through the entire process as a family, from choosing and photographing the shirts to listing them on a website and then finally to attempting to sell them and ship them out. Our kids were still fairly young, but they experienced the risk and the complete unknown. Would the shirts actually sell? Or would we just waste a lot of money?

We were thrilled when our first run of T-shirts was a success. This set the stage for all that was to come, although we didn't know it yet. When our T-shirt supply ran low, we ordered more. When we messed up orders by sending the wrong size (which happened more than we were anticipating), we ordered more. These reorders came extremely quickly—in just a day or two.

As the months went on, our reorders started to come in less and less quickly. What used to take three or four days turned into five or six, and then sometimes over a week. Finally, I asked what was going on. How come our shirts used to come in so quickly and now they were taking much longer?

With all our children gathered around, the man who was making all our T-shirts told us that when the COVID pandemic shut down the world, most of his work went with it. He had been making apparel for sports teams and school events. That business disappeared. As time progressed, his regular flow of work was beginning to pick back up again. He ended his explanation by telling us that it was our business that had kept his business afloat during those trying times.

The point here is that we never know when this one step will lead to that next step, or when this brick is laying the foundation for that brick. We never know how our bravery or our response to our own calling will intersect with the lives of others, lifting everyone up at the same time.

I know so much more about life now than when I first read that passage by John Holt. I learned that beautiful unknowns await us when we try new things. There is mystery out there. There are untold stories waiting for their grand finale. There are floors to be swept and chickens to be saved, businesses to start and beds to be made.

The glory of all of it is that, as homeschoolers, you get to do it together. Because you are all homeschoolers. It's not just the kids. You're learning too. And somehow, all of that adds up to more than the sum of its parts.

It is difficult to explain that by choosing what seems on the surface to be the more time-consuming decision—taking on the full weight of our kids' education—we all come out better for it in the end. But this is how growth works. We experience growth by choosing something unknown and a little scary.

If I weren't writing this book, I'd be grading math papers. They'd be similar to the math papers I graded last week, last year, last decade. I was better at that than I am at writing. But those math papers did not open up my world like homeschooling has. These lessons I've learned firsthand over many years now are shared experiences, enriching both my life and my children's. As you model to your family how to craft a life, you are doing homeschooling right.

# 6

## You Are Requiring Self-Reliance

The people who are horrified by the idea of children learning what they want to learn when they want to learn it have not accepted the very elementary psychological fact that people (all people, of every age) remember the things that are important to them—the things they *need to know*—and forget the rest.

—Daniel Quinn[1]

Nobody wants to do math. Nobody wants to do much of what I want them to do, really.

So, over the years, I became a broken record. I would cajole and attempt to convince our kids, who had never known anything but homeschooling, that the forced schoolwork they were doing was so much less than their public school counterparts', and shouldn't they be oh so grateful. I would say things like, "If you were in the school building down the road, this would last seven hours instead of two, and then they would send you more work to do at home in the afternoon and on the weekends." Eight thousand times I said this.

That approach doesn't work.

Namely because kids have the capacity to do a remarkable job driving their own education, and also because most people, if we're being honest, don't want to be told what to do—though sometimes it is necessary.

But still, I did want our kids to finish their math pages, and I didn't want to have to work so hard at convincing them to do it. I devised a plan.

"Tomorrow," I announced, "we will begin running a simulation of a full day of school, complete with a bus ride and homework. It will last two days. That way you'll sort of experience what it's really like."

Wide eyes turned my way as I laid down some ground rules: "In the morning, you will need to be ready to go by 8:00. That means you will have to be fully dressed, have your hair and teeth brushed, and have eaten breakfast and packed a lunch before we get on the bus (the couch) for forty-five minutes. I'll expect you to refer to me as 'Mrs. Yurich' once you get off the bus (the couch)."

Then I proceeded to create a morning for them that was similar to the kindergarten class I substitute taught all those years ago. Each minute was filled and directed. It wasn't awful. Some, though not all, of the work was engaging enough. We had a potty break. For the most part, the morning was quiet—filled with sounds of pencil to paper, some further instruction, and not much else. It wasn't very vibrant, but it was fine.

Around 11:30, we broke for forty-five minutes for a combo of lunch and recess. This was when the boisterous sounds began. Our kids seemed to come alive instantly. That forty-five minutes flew by, and then I had to call all of them in from outside, where they had found delight and were getting along perfectly well. I certainly interrupted whatever they had decided to do out there. Calling them back sliced a knife through their intentions.

It was then that I heard a phrase I'd never heard any of my kids utter before.

"What should we do next, Mrs. Yurich?"

And I would never be the same again.

We quit once those words were said. I had planned to finish out the afternoon in a fashion similar to the morning and have them plop back on the "bus" for their forty-five-minute ride "home," with homework in hand. But this little simulation I had contrived for the sake of my kids turned out to be mostly for my own benefit because, in a decade of home educating, no one had ever asked me what to do next. And one half day of simulated, forced schooling changed that.

I realized that for all the annoyances I went through in a typical day of homeschooling, wading through a fairly messy, loud house, this simple environment we were providing had given our children a huge gift that I didn't know they had. They could structure their own time. They weren't reliant or waiting on me to tell them what to do. Sure, I occasionally stepped in with directions, but they often bemoaned that because they were already following their own internal guide.

Certainly, there are times in life when we must comply and get on board. But for the rest of it, our wild insides can lead us if we're used to listening.

I want to say that homeschooled kids learn self-reliance over the years, but I think it's more accurate to say that they never lost it. What parent kneels down on the floor next to their seven-month-old and begins doling out instructions on how to crawl?

## How to Be Good at Life

We look at childhood and equate much of it to becoming educated. But what does that even mean? Does it mean you can quote Shakespeare, locate Madagascar on a map, or determine the area of a trapezoid?

How to become an "educated" person is at the heart of what we're doing with kids—whether they are at home or in an institutionalized setting—yet often we don't stop to truly consider what we're after. Is it a high SAT score? College scholarships? Ivy League acceptance? Or are we looking beyond those things? A stable job? A home with a pool and a waterslide?

So I pause and look at my own life. More than likely, I'm somewhere around halfway through. What do I want? What does being educated mean to me? If it means that I can quote Shakespeare, locate Madagascar on a map, and determine the area of a trapezoid, I would fail. At one point in my life, I was teaching others the formula for how to calculate the area of a trapezoid. But I don't remember that anymore.

I want some stability. I want fulfillment. And I want deep relationships. These things have not sprung out of a typical K–12 education. In fact, quite the opposite.

Schooling seems to almost promise future success. Do X, Y, and Z ad nauseam for thirteen years and you will be saved. As will your children and your children's children. Ivan Illich wrote, "School leaves them (our kids) with the expectation (or counterfeit hope) that their grandchildren will make it."[2]

When I was on the verge of leaving a thirteen-year system of being told what to do most days, I felt lost. How could I have felt any differently? Thirteen years is a long time spent learning that someone else should be at the helm of our lives, directing it this way and that.

I stayed the course. I continued my education and then ended up right back where I started, in a classroom. It was only when I stepped away from all of that that my life began to flourish. Expansion happened because of forced growth. Forced growth happened because I left what I knew to become a mother.

My true life's education began when those two lines showed up on the pregnancy test. That was when I began learning for the sake of bettering my life. And I know beyond knowing that if I had taken my six weeks at home and gone back to the classroom, I would've prevented what turned out to be the precipice of life change: spending my days in a sea of the unknown.

My learning outside of school began when I needed to know things for the sake of life enhancement. Becoming a parent forced me to finally dig into things like learning to cook (I'm still not very good at it), structuring a life, making a little extra money on the side, and most importantly, trying to learn the point of it all.

As homeschooling families, we've set out on a journey in which we don't know where the finish line is. That finish line may include knowledge of Shakespeare, a deep understanding of geography or geometry, or something else completely.

Alfie Kohn put it this way on his website: "Dewey reminded us that the goal of education is more education. To be well educated, then, is to have the desire as well as the means to make sure learning never ends."[3]

How interesting. The goal of education is not some slip of paper that announces you are educated; rather, it is a lifestyle of continued learning for the sake of growth and enjoyment, both of which contribute to a rich and fulfilling life.

## A Global Pandemic

That COVID-19 pandemic derailed me. Others seem to have gotten over it. We are still reeling a bit over here. I've never quite regained a sense of how I felt before. Life seems more tippy, less certain.

Looking through some of the screenshots on my phone takes me back. An announcement from a local college on March 11, 2020, said this:

> As the spread of the coronavirus (COVID-19) continues, our top priority continues to be the health and safety of the CMU community. There are currently no known cases of COVID-19 at CMU, but as announced early this morning, there are now two confirmed cases in Michigan.
>
> Out of an abundance of caution, and to prevent and contain the spread of the coronavirus, all CMU classes will move online after spring break through March 20.[4]

Comments and advice began to spring up everywhere online. I was gathering tips from the bowels of the internet:

> Wear a mask, wear eye protection, and if you don't have those, go to the supermarket when it's least crowded.

The surfaces of food will be contaminated. Buy long-lasting foods, bring them home, leave them for ten days on the floor or in a separate room—that's enough time for the virus to disappear on its own.

Coronavirus will have a hard time thriving in the nose, mouth, or lungs of someone who chews raw, crushed garlic daily.

Little did I know that while we were quarantining our groceries and chomping on garlic cloves, things would still be raging on in Michigan six months, a year, even eighteen months later. We could never have foreseen, for instance, that taking two weeks to flatten the curve would morph into shutting down tubing on an outdoor river almost six months later:

The popular attraction along the Huron River, featuring a series of drop pools that typically draw crowds in the summer, is off limits to tubers in the interest of public health amid the COVID-19 pandemic, officials said. The decision is in line with emergency orders enacted by the Washtenaw County Health Department and City Council to limit the size of outdoor gatherings to 25 people.[5]

The pandemic altered the meaning of true education for me. We had to adapt. We also had to think critically. Yes, tubing down a river could be considered an outdoor gathering. I guess. But I've never in my life seen twenty-five or more people connected, tubing down a river. This interpretation of "emergency orders" was bizarre, to put it mildly.

This experience underscored something I now know for sure: The capacity to think critically and adapt doesn't arise from seatwork. Ever. It emerges from facing new challenges, walking through the unknown, and learning from trial and experience. Working through that discomfort shows us we can navigate uncharted waters, both literally and figuratively.

Michael Easter writes about our natural inclinations to choose comfort and safety in his book *The Comfort Crisis*. We mistakenly view a comfy, cushy life as an end goal, but we never arrive at that goal because, as Easter explains, our brains adapt, we get used to our easier surroundings, and then we crave even more comfort.

If someone magically arrived here from the 1800s, they would be mesmerized by a washing machine or a dishwasher, but no one today is mesmerized by these machines. They are commonplace. We don't forever remain enthralled with advancements and discoveries. This is by design. Complacency doesn't lead to innovation. Our brains get used to the status quo and get moving on to something else. Easter refers to this phenomenon as "problem creep."

"As we experience fewer problems," he writes, "we don't become more satisfied. We just lower our threshold for what we consider a problem. We end up with the same number of troubles. Except our new problems are progressively more hollow."[6]

The finish lines in our lives are always moving. We cannot change this. Our brains adjust our goals automatically. Therefore, being educated is not some static thing; it's not a finite accomplishment.

Part of being educated is knowing what to do next. Or at least being willing and having both the skills and the bravery to try to figure out what's next. Education encompasses knowing how to fix our mistakes and mend our hurts.

The global pandemic took summer tubing off the table (a minor inconvenience) but also led to some career upheaval, and I found myself at the helm of a global platform aimed at getting kids outside, families connected, and screens less in the forefront. The problem was, and still is, that I have no idea what I'm doing. I don't know a thing about running a business, marketing, or even writing books, for that matter.

Daily, my insides scream at me. No one is telling me what to do, and yet I have to do something. I have to confront what I don't know. All those years of being given assignments and completing assignments, taking tests and being assessed, did not prepare me for these adjustments I am continually making as I try to weave my way through a vast unknown.

The truly incredible part is that I've gotten to learn what is on the other side of uncertainty. In our case, it includes a number-one mobile app, a top-ranked podcast, conversations with authors I never could've imagined speaking with, travels around the country, bestselling books, and so much more. A prescribed life was much more limiting. My current life is harder and scarier but also fulfilling. I am stretched daily, and my education—my pursuit to becoming educated—is clearly a lifelong journey.

## Good Students Wait

John Taylor Gatto wrote an essay about some of the messages that children absorb through an industrialized school system. One thing they learn is this: "Good students wait for a teacher to tell them what to do. This is the most important lesson of them all: we must wait for other people, better trained than ourselves, to make the meanings of our lives."[7] The teachers hold the keys to the locks that they've deemed important (or have been assigned).

When you home educate, the world opens up for your children. They no longer have to wait. Life is at their fingertips.

If you attended school in a traditional setting, you can recall how much of your time there was spent waiting. You waited to be told what to do, when to do it, and how to do it. You waited when other students were being disciplined. You waited for other students to finish before you could go on. You waited at the end of tests and quizzes. You waited in line. You waited for your turn to be called on. You waited to start your life.

A dear friend of ours is a producer and songwriter for some of the world's most popular music. When he reminisces on his school days, he recalls that it was pretty much all waiting. Every day he was waiting to leave so he could get home to his first love, songwriting. The songs wove through his brain all day long, but school made him wait for an opportune time to go after what he was really interested in.

This stands in contrast to Chef Nathan Lippy's childhood experience. Chef Nathan currently works for Blackstone as their brand chef, content creator, director of content and strategy, and so many other things. His childhood was also filled with dreaming, but his days included a whole lot of doing what he loved because he was homeschooled. Nathan told me about how he cooked his first three-course dinner for his mom and some of her friends when he was around twelve and made ravioli from scratch around age ten, after being inspired by chefs he loved like early Emeril Lagasse,

Martha Stewart, Sara Moulton, Graham Kerr, and Julia Child. He was obsessed, just as so many children are about their personal passions, and he had the time and freedom to follow his obsession.

The first thing Chef Nathan ever cooked on his own was a Martha Stewart dish, a basic 3-2-1 pasta recipe. He used that pasta dish to make homemade ravioli that he filled with some leftover queso the family had in the fridge. He used a fork to press around the edges, par-cooked them in water, and then finished the cooking in a sauté pan with butter and garlic—just like Martha!

His mom came home to a massive mess. There was flour everywhere from this homemade pasta escapade. He called it the "Ten-Year-Old Aftermath." So a young Chef Nathan— this homeschooled fourth grader who had the competency and freedom to get out ingredients and try something real, to boil and fry—set to clearing up the kitchen while his mom tried his dish. His first attempt.

Chef Nathan reported, "My mom sat down to eat, and I remember the look on her face changed my life. 'You made this?' she asked. 'How did you do this? This is amazing.'

"She was so happy with what I had created," he told me. And immediately, he knew: "That's what I want to do for the rest of my life. I want to serve people like that."[8]

Both Chef Nathan and our songwriter friend love their jobs. Both men ended up in careers they are passionate about. Yet their childhoods were vastly different. One involved waiting; the other involved doing.

Logistically, there just isn't time for the doing when thirty-five-plus hours of some of the best parts of the week go to drudgery, week in and week out. Kids come home from their days at school exhausted and spent. They've lost so much of their passion simply because they are tired. Because they've had to wait and wait. Is that a death sentence? No. Clearly, many people who spent a good portion of their childhoods with their bottoms in a seat go on to do great things. But life is not just about the destination. It's about the path to get there.

Homeschooled kids wait only for themselves. They have the opportunity to go after life with abandon, learning what they love and what they loathe through experience. They hit the ground running long before adulthood, long before they receive a rolled-up piece of paper that denotes an education.

Austin Kleon promotes a fascinating kind of learning that could be adapted for anyone: "Find the influences that influenced the person that's influencing you."[9]

If you're inspired by Alexander Graham Bell, C. S. Lewis, Frederick Douglass, Rosa Parks, Bessie Coleman, Gordon Ramsay, Dave Ramsey, Serena Williams, Jennifer Lopez, Elvis Presley, Marie Curie, or Pablo Picasso, then learn about them. But go further. Learn where they got their inspiration from.

Heather LeFebvre, creator of The Nature Journaler, does something similar. Heather has studied in-depth how nature has influenced different famous writers. She looks into the surrounding environments and countrysides where they grew up and offers an online class called "Nature & Nurture: Jane Austen, the Brontës, and Beatrix Potter." Heather describes what you will learn this way: "In this class we will spend six weeks immersed in the nature that surrounded and inspired the lives of Jane Austen, Charlotte, Emily, and Anne Brontë, and Beatrix Potter. We will discover how deeply nature influenced them as persons and as writers. We will use these discoveries to guide our own nature exploration and nature journaling."[10]

What a fascinating approach to learning about the authors you love. Through these types of studies, Heather speaks on how she developed a rich understanding of those who influenced her. The conversation that we had oozed education. She told me about Jane Austen and how she spent most of her life in the county of Hampshire in southern England, where she was surrounded by farmland and wealthy estates. She helped in her own family's garden and on their family farm, but she also had opportunities to stay in the homes of the wealthy and experience their gorgeous gardens.

Through her studies of what has influenced the writers she admires, Heather learned that there have been different nature trends through the centuries. In the Jane Austen era, the British began taking walking trips to see picturesque areas that had a Gothic feel to them, like ruined castles.

Heather went on to describe how Beatrix Potter, who has created such beautiful artwork steeped in nature, didn't get to be outside much as a child because her mother kept her locked in the top floor of their London house. This type of childhood led Beatrix to crave nature. So much so that she saved her money and purchased her own farm, far from London. So many homes are steeped in the drawings of Beatrix Potter.

Heather spoke of Louisa May Alcott and her difficult life. Louisa never married and spent most of her adulthood trying to support her parents and sisters. Nature was her solace. And then, get this: Louisa May Alcott once took a summer class about wildflowers with Henry David Thoreau.

Heather also described how C. S. Lewis would take yearly holidays and go out to remote places to walk. He and his friends would walk during the day, spend the night in a pub, and continue on with their walking the following day. Lewis was heavily influenced by nature. One of his early memories was of a tiny fairy garden that his brother made in a little tin can that Lewis was enamored with. That little tin garden and Beatrix Potter's book *The Tale of Squirrel Nutkin* were influences on his life. These authors influenced each other. "They didn't just come out of a vacuum," Heather said. What an enthralling learning path for Heather to walk down, doing a deep dive into whatever inspires her.

Like Chef Nathan, Heather was homeschooled. She spent a lot of her time during her middle school years on calligraphy. She practiced on her own, and to this day, calligraphy is an integral part of her beautiful nature journaling.

Homeschooling, far from being merely an educational choice, is a profound act of faith in the natural capabilities of our children and ourselves. This journey isn't about ticking boxes or following a prescribed path to academic success; it's about trusting in the inherent curiosity and capacity for self-guidance that every child possesses. Homeschooling strips away the external pressures and distractions that often cloud traditional educational settings, allowing children the space to explore, learn, and grow at their own pace and in their own way.

## The Path Forward

In choosing to homeschool, you have taken a bold step toward nurturing a unique and profound kind of education—one that extends far beyond the confines of traditional classroom walls. This journey is not just about academic achievement; it's about fostering self-reliance, encouraging curiosity, and nurturing a lifelong love of learning.

The stories and insights in this chapter underscore a vital message: Homeschooling can foster a rich environment where children actively participate in crafting their own educational journeys rather than passively receiving knowledge. Whether it's Chef Nathan finding his passion in the kitchen or your own children discovering the joy of self-directed learning, the benefits of this approach are clear. You are encouraging your children to engage deeply with their interests, leading to a more profound and personal connection with the world around them. This isn't mere preparation for life; it's living fully. Education is seamlessly integrated into the daily fabric of life, supporting a lifelong love of learning.

Homeschooling is more than a form of education; it's a lifestyle choice that embraces the unpredictable, the spontaneous, and the joyously serendipitous aspects of learning. It is a bold step toward a future where education is not confined to the walls of a classroom but is a continuous, dynamic journey that occurs everywhere, at all times. As homeschoolers, parents are not just educators; they are facilitators of a vast, exciting world that their children are eager to explore.

So, homeschool parents, know this: Each day you choose this path, you aren't only teaching your children; you are giving them the tools and empowering them to teach themselves, to discover their passions, and to pursue a life of rich and rewarding learning. You are crafting the innovative thinkers, the creative problem solvers, and the passionate leaders of the future. Your dedication and trust in this process form the cornerstone of a truly educated, deeply connected, and profoundly capable individual. Your moments of doubt will be overshadowed by countless moments of discovery, joy, and profound growth—both for you and for your children. You are indeed doing it right, far beyond what you might realize.

# You Are Offering Freedom

Movement and play profoundly improve—not only learn-ing—but creativity, stress management, and health.

—Carla Hannaford, *Smart Moves*[1]

Noticing so many swing sets, playgrounds, and forest trails void of kids was the impetus for coining the phrase "1000 Hours Outside." For two years, our family spent large swaths of time underneath the Michigan sun and clouds, doing what looked like a whole bunch of "nothing" that, as it turned out, offered a great deal of long-lasting developmental benefits. Not only had time in nature benefited my own mental health and well-being; it simultaneously dumped loads of benefits on our children as well.

I felt pressure from the very beginning to enroll our chil-dren in structured programs. I couldn't pinpoint where that pressure came from exactly, but it just seemed to be swirling in the atmosphere. No one I knew was simply letting their kids loose in the forest to pick up acorns or meander down trails. Instead, we were scouring the internet and our local parks and recreation quarterly brochures for places where we could sign up. Signing up also meant, in many cases, forking over money—which we didn't have much of at the time.

On the surface, childhood freedoms seem to be the enemy. Kids are wild banshees. They have an unfathomable amount of energy. They are irrational and pushy. Even at an early age when they can hardly express themselves with words, they know what they want, and they know how to wail to get it. Surely we shouldn't put them in charge of anything, much less leave them alone for hours at a time, right?

And yet, our hovering, our fixing, our structuring, and our scheduling—to the extent that it undermines a child's will and direction—are leading to a silent crisis that goes unnoticed as we happily shell out more and more money for different types of adult-led enrichment opportunities. We flip through the catalogs of enticing activities, from field hockey to martial arts to music to swimming, and all we can see are the benefits. Of course those are all we see. No program owner or coordinator in their right mind would include the downsides in their advertisement. *Learn violin but miss family dinners! Pick up a second or a third language at the expense of open-ended play!* A significant reduction in play and freedom has silently slipped past us, I believe in part because we never fully understood the benefits of those things in the first place.

## Historical Context

Mothers in previous generations who didn't enroll their child in all the after-school programming didn't do so because they were well-versed in the benefits of open-ended play during childhood. They skipped out of those activities because they simply didn't exist to the extent that they do today. Many families didn't have the money or the resources to accommodate all the programs that we overschedule children with today. The cultural norm was after-school play, not after-school participation in programs.

It takes time to see that childhood freedom pays off. The logical mind doesn't grasp how the seemingly disorganized and random play of a child could possibly be the best-case scenario. But when a parent gives their child a day, a week, or months of freedom at a time, like during a summer break from school, a thriving child emerges. The child who spends the afternoons and summers in abounding freedom of choice—with the wind in their hair, the sun in their eyes, and sticks in their hands—is an exuberant child. The parent sees that. They live in a home with children who, for the most part, eat well, sleep well, and are happily exhausted at the end of each day.

It used to be common to experience childhood in this way, as a result of cultural norms and how society was structured. In general, family sizes were larger, disposable income was lower, and transportation wasn't as readily available.

Let's kick off this discussion with average family size. In 1800, women had an average of seven kids. Over the past two hundred years, that number has been decreasing, as we are all well aware. Though some families these days might still have seven (or more) children, by 2018 women in the United States had an average of less than two kids.[2]

Let's talk about my own five kids. We're at a number that is a little under average compared to those mamas who lived in the 1800s but above average compared to today's families. Even if I really wanted my kids in more programming, the cost to enroll all of them in the Pirate Summer Camp program available in our school district would be more than $200 per day (and that's with a sibling discount). Do the math. That's $4,000 per month, plus an annual $75 registration fee. For some perspective, when I first started my teaching job in the early 2000s, my two-week paychecks were less than $1,000. I made less than $2,000 per month starting my life out as a professional woman. I set that lucrative income aside when we had kids and I chose to stay home, and now I had $0 per month on my own to put toward enticing programs like Pirate Summer Camp.

Once again, the bygone generations had more kids and less disposable income. This was not true for every family, but the general trend was part of the driving force behind why kids played in neighborhoods in the afternoons. And speaking of driving, it wasn't until 1980 that two- or three-car households even became the norm. In 1960, only 19% of households in the United States had two cars, and 2.5% of families had three cars. Around 20% of families would have had personal transportation throughout the day to get to places like an additional job or extracurricular activities. One decade later, in 1970, 29.3% of households had two cars, and 5.5% owned three or more vehicles.[3]

Are you seeing the change? Within a span of ten years, the number of families who were more homebound, living much of their lives within a small radius, had shrunk. We were nearing a tipping point.

That point came in 1980, when more than 50% of households had two vehicles (34%) or more (17.5%).[4]

This increase in transportation options enabled families to begin shuttling kids around to after-school activities. And as family size decreased, gone also were the afternoon hours when (usually) the mother was found at home because she had to cook a meal for dinner. Spending after-school hours driving kids from activity to activity hadn't been a possibility when a family of six, seven, or more people would need to eat within the next few hours.

My husband's grandma grew up in the 1940s and 1950s. She told me about a family in her neighborhood that had seventeen children. They had a system of filling the beds in the house depending on when they were ready to go to sleep at night. In other words, beds were not personal spaces but were communal and solely served their primary function of providing a spot to sleep. Surely only the wealthiest of the wealthy would be able to send kids from a family of that size to a summer day camp. Today, that would cost almost $700 per day, and that includes the sibling discount!

One of the biggest questions we should be asking ourselves is, "What if this shift toward adult-directed childhoods didn't derive from research regarding what's best for children, but instead came out of a lack of understanding regarding what to do with extra monetary resources and access to more transportation?"

We can and should still learn from families who had fewer resources yet still managed to weave fulfilling lives for themselves. If we are making our decisions based on what everyone around us seems to be doing, we might be following a cultural phenomenon that isn't truly considering the needs of the child. Take a moment to review your children's daily schedule. Are there opportunities to reduce structured activities and allow more time for freedom? Consider eliminating one or two activities to make room for self-structured time.

## Neighborhood Play

One of the things we can do as homeschooling families is create child-centered play environments around where we live. Mike Lanza is an expert on creating "Playborhoods," neighborhoods that draw from the types of experiences of the past that provided the structures needed for childhood play. As homeschoolers begin to spend more and more time in spaces that used to be teeming with kids, such as neighborhoods and playgrounds, we affect more than just our own family. The benefits of less-structured childhoods permeate outward into the larger community.

The more kids there are playing at a particular place, the more inviting that environment will be to other children. The lure of other kids will help pull children away from the lure of screens and lead to independent, spontaneous play. So how can we design or redesign our environments to prioritize freedom, play, and child-led leisure? Is there currently anything in our environments that is enticing children to explore, or do we need to purposefully add some of that in?

Mike's observations of daily life highlight a disturbing trend where "children are often transported from one structured activity to another, with neighborhoods that once buzzed with the noise of play now silent and empty."[5]

The impetus is on our shoulders to find ways to create spaces in childhood that are vibrant hubs of activity. When these don't exist, a vicious cycle emerges. If there is no one to play with, no one wants to go play. The number of over-scheduled kids decreases the number of playmates available for the kids who are around and ready to make up games or play pretend with others. While childhood used to include endless hours of imaginative dialogue, a society overflowing with adult-directed opportunities for kids quickly hampers the social and developmental opportunities for all.

Mike offers an interesting suggestion to start turning the needle back toward how things once were. Make your neighborhood more engaging by placing playthings in the front yard, instead of behind privacy fences and out of sight in the backyard. Mike did just that! He filled his front yard with a variety of creative installations like sandboxes, play rivers, and interactive mosaics—all designed to entice a broad age range and encourage spontaneous interaction among neighborhood kids. His idea is to entice not just children who are the same age but kids of all ages. This is directly in line with the advice of Dr. Peter Gray, who advocates for multi-age play as a driver for learning throughout childhood.

Mike does a fabulous job accounting for different types of living situations in his book *Playborhood*.[6] Obviously, not everyone lives in a neighborhood with a front yard and can do the things just described. The general principle of seeing other children play, however, still holds true. Think about how you can accomplish this where you live. Is there a courtyard in your apartment complex in which you can add some open-ended materials? Can you frequent the neighborhood park in your city a little more often? When you invite other children over to play, can you kindly keep them off screens and instead engaged in hands-on experience?

Allowing children the liberty to explore and engage with their environment cultivates skills such as risk-taking and independence. By aiming to appeal to our children's desire for adventure, we can increase the likelihood that they will choose the unpredictable joys of outdoor play over the predictable allure of digital screens.

The classroom is not a playground. I heard this over and over again as a child. Neither are so many of the indoor spaces we often take children to, like church, the library, the grocery store, and doctors' appointments. If we begin to view our neighborhoods as places to restore children's agency in their own leisure, we can set a foundation for healthier and more fulfilling lives. Because we homeschool, this outlook can begin right in our very homes.

## Play Deprivation

The research decrying the detriments of too much structure in childhood has been pouring in over the past few decades as we have seen an overall restructuring of childhood. We are running ourselves and our kids ragged, while simultaneously seeing the alarming consequences that arise from play deprivation.

Angela Hanscom, a noted expert on child development, pointed out to me that this modern way of raising children, in which they sometimes sit for up to nine hours in a day, is restricting not only their physical development but also their neurological development, amid many other unintended consequences.[7]

Freedom of movement gives children the ability to navigate their environments safely as they develop a good sense of body awareness. Lack of activity leads to shortened muscles that shouldn't be shortened.

Unstructured play, especially play that occurs outside, has a vital role in developing the vestibular sense, which integrates sensory experiences. Playgrounds were once havens of joyous abandon, but they have been scaled back, with shorter slides and swings. Many of these changes have occurred due to litigation, but there are consequences to those changes. The shorter swings and slides reduce the amount of sensory input a child can experience while using them, and loads of sensory input is essential for optimal growth throughout childhood.

Merry-go-rounds, another former playground staple, provide powerful vestibular input through centrifugal force, but they have also been removed. Angela says, "These changes are not trivial; they represent a significant barrier to children's natural growth and sensory needs, which are instinctively tuned to seek out necessary developmental activities."[8]

It is often the types of movements that might make adults feel uneasy—such as spinning, swinging, and rolling—that actually are critical for strengthening all six of the eye muscles, enhancing visual coordination. Furthermore, when kids are allowed to fidget and move freely, they are better able to focus and pay attention for extended periods. Go figure. Your squirrelly child knows innately that movement helps them learn better. This reflects a fundamental mismatch between an adult-imposed structure and the intrinsic needs of the child's neurological system, which thrives on varied, novel stimuli found in unstructured outdoor environments.

I talked about this with Sarah Mackenzie, founder of Read-Aloud Revival.[9] She touts the myriad benefits of reading aloud to our children throughout the entirety of their childhoods, even (long) after they have the ability to read to themselves. But it is a myth, Sarah explains, that children must be sitting still while we read aloud to them. "For some kids, information can go deeper into their brains when the child physically moves around," she writes in *The Read-Aloud Family*.[10]

Biologist and award-winning educator Carla Hannaford told me plain and simple, "Kids cannot learn sitting still and being quiet."[11] In fact, she recounted the story of a woman who took one of her college courses and never took a single note from any of the lectures. Instead, this woman spent every lecture knitting a sweater. Carla chuckled as she remembered that not only did this student end up completing the course with one of the highest grades in the class, but she also ended up with a brand-new sweater.

Carla has woven together much of the science that ties movement to learning. Beyond this, she teaches that when we move, we actually grow more mitochondria in our bodies. Often we feel tired not because we are moving too much but because we aren't moving enough!

Children are innately wired to move, so when they are taken out of a classroom setting, they move more. This is obvious. A classroom setting intrinsically de-emphasizes movement because children are confined to desks much of the day. Even if they are given a flexible or bouncy seat to sit on, it isn't feasible for a child to move their body in complex ways when there are a dozen or more other children in this confined space. The classroom does not facilitate the kinds of movements that kids are naturally drawn to.

At home, however, the possibilities for movement open up. Of course, there is more time to spend outdoors, but even indoors, children find creative ways to move their bodies. They balance on things. They hang upside down from couches. In some homes, parents install hand swings or chin-up bars in doorways. They hang hammocks under tables for kids to read in. You can invest in movement opportunities within your home, but as biomechanist Katy Bowman says, "The biggest piece of exercise equipment we are ignoring is our floor."

She asked me, "Want to get your heart rate up? No need for fancy cardio equipment. Begin by standing and then get down to the ground, ending up face down . . . then face up. . . . Repeat this cycle five to ten times. It's more fatiguing than you think. Bodies are big weights. Getting up and down from the floor is like a whole-body bicep curl."[12]

All this movement helps children develop their proprioceptive sense as well. Proprioceptive activities—such as pushing, pulling, and digging—provide the necessary resistance kids need to help develop joint and muscle health and overall body awareness. These activities are not just forms of play; they are vital for kids to be able to regulate their responses to sensory inputs. While it may not seem like a huge deal, the ability to regulate responses to stimuli contributes to overall emotional and physical regulation.

## Time for Exploration

I read *The Midnight Library*[13] earlier this year. The book is about the ripple effects of different life choices. It brought me a lot of solace as a theme emerged that deviating from a plan may actually turn out better, although there is also the possibility that things will turn out worse.

I was passionate about teaching from an early age. When I was twelve, I started working with children at my family's church, teaching the three-year-olds' class during Vacation

155

Bible School. This experience sparked a path that would see me teaching private piano lessons in our home for $5 per lesson in the 1990s, then teaching swim lessons at a local pool for several summers, and ultimately starting a career teaching in a classroom.

In my later years of high school, I had to set aside my passion for teaching due to time constraints. But my love for music remained strong. I'd started playing the piano at the age of four, and my journey took me from timidly hiding under the piano bench during lessons when I was just starting out, to studying under the head of the piano department at the University of Michigan School of Music. I had to audition for the opportunity, and I was one of only two students younger than college age permitted to take lessons with the department head without being officially enrolled in the university.

I'll never forget walking into that audition with renowned, award-winning professor Lynne Bartholomew. Her office held not just one but two concert grand pianos, a mahogany desk, and shelves filled with books. I learned so much from her. I grew in my skills immensely over the course of a few years. I was a shoo-in for the University of Michigan college music program because, even though I would still have to audition, Lynne would be the one helping me prepare.

But a rift began to develop in my soul. The level of preparation for these weekly lessons increased. I was supposed to come each week with all the piano scores memorized. She was looking for a few hours of practice a day, which at my stage of life as a public school kid was astronomical. But to my kids, it would be a drop in the bucket.

We created a symphony together on those grand pianos, Lynne and I. She sat at one, and I sat at the other. We played Rachmaninoff and Chopin, Czerny and Debussy. She let me in on master classes with some of the college students, as well as performances where I got to sit right next to her and turn the pages while she accompanied some ensemble or another.

It was the eleventh-grade workload that did me in. This is a path I never let my brain go down until now, and it's emotional. My workload included a mix of five or six rigorous courses at a time that sent me home with untold amounts of homework and exams to study for. This was also the age when I got a "real" job, as the rat at Chuck E. Cheese. I still taught a few piano lessons in our home, but I also added a steady stream of income by throwing birthday parties for screaming children while dressed up in the hotbox of that rat costume.

It was in this busyness that I lost my first love. It was a slow fizzle out. I showed up week after week to that glorious room filled to the brim with pianos, and I was less and less prepared.

I am satisfied with where I am in life, but an "if only" lives within the deep recesses of my mind.

If only I hadn't felt pressured to take such rigorous courses for the sake of my future.

If only the teachers hadn't given so much homework.

If only the tests hadn't demanded so much of me in terms of preparation.

If only I had been just a little smarter and the material all came easier to me.

If only GPA didn't matter so much.

If only I had had more time or knew how to better manage my time.

All the studying and preparation that were supposed to lead me down a prescribed path toward the right future actually took me farther from my dreams. I was just a hop, skip, and jump away from landing with Lynne long-term, and yet it didn't seem prudent to let any of the plates drop that included acronyms like AP, SAT, and GPA.

Alfie Kohn writes about the idiocy of having children prepare for certain tests because the more we do this, "the less meaningful the results of the test." He poses a question that is worth pondering: "Astute parents and other observers will then ask, 'How much time was sacrificed from real learning just so kids could get better at taking the [name of test]?'"[14]

I was at an end-of-year vocal performance at Michigan State University earlier this spring, and I sat right in front of the accompanying pianist, filled with emotion. Could that have been me? Did the trappings of an institutional K–12 education prepare me to be brave, to shirk off labels and chase that life I really wanted? Or did it scream at me to be more cautious? Don't veer. Don't let your grades drop. Spend your time with all this material that will be of no consequence to you in the next few years, or months, or weeks, or even days.

I remember sitting with my guidance counselor a handful of times throughout my public high school career. In retrospect, what she and the entire educational system handed me was a narrow view of life. My situation is common.

Ryan and Hannah Maruyama talk about this on their *Degree Free* podcast. Hannah explains that teenagers and young adults often aren't aware of the full range of career paths available to them. The common narrative suggests only a few options: purchasing a college degree, entering the trades, or joining the military. Yet this overlooks numerous other possibilities. Many don't realize they could pursue careers in technology, human resources, sales, or even "craft work, which is different from trade work."[15] The scope of opportunities open to them is far broader than they realize.

Most eye-opening to me was what Hannah said about the teenagers she works with as a coach and mentor: "A lot of these teens and young adults can only name six to eight jobs total. And it's almost always the same exact jobs because of that. The options they know of are very limited, and something you and I talk about a lot is the fact that they can't walk through a door if they don't know that door exists."[16]

I relate. By the time I neared the end of my K–12 career, I knew only a few things about myself as it would relate to a career. I was good at math. I still played the piano but had stepped away from lessons. And I liked kids. So I became a math teacher.

I have since learned that there are scores of jobs you can get when you enjoy math. I didn't know they existed. And my life was so full that I didn't have the time to pursue the options.

According to CBS News, "In 2023, the share of jobs on hiring platform ZipRecruiter that listed a bachelor's degree as a requirement dropped to 14.5%, from 18% in 2022."[17]

The way we launch into adulthood can carry a lot of lifelong implications. When kids are run ragged from excessive amounts of schoolwork, extracurriculars, youth sports, and jobs, there is little time left over to reflect. If only 14.5% of job postings require a bachelor's degree, does it make sense to always be chasing that? Or can some of this precious childhood time when we can dream and ponder be shifted toward different goals?

## Play as a Teenager

Play as a teenager looks different from play as a young child, but it is no less important. It should still involve large swaths of time that are given to open-ended experiences. It's in those times that kids gain enough self-knowledge and self-awareness to kick off their adult lives. Instead of just hopping into the current, there is time to mess around with some of the different options out there and to reflect on those experiences.

I took a career-type quiz during high school and was given a sheet of paper with a short list of results on it. I truly had no idea that possibilities existed beyond being a teacher, nurse, or dentist—those types of jobs.

Number-one bestselling author and career expert Ken Coleman offers a more comprehensive type of career assessment than the one I took during high school. You can find it in his book *Find the Work You're Wired to Do*.[18] He offers a version for students and for adults. I took the adult version, and it gave me insight not only on what I do best (my talents) but also on what I really love and enjoy (my passions) and what I care deeply about (my mission). Ken says that when we combine these three pillars—talent, passion, and mission—we will have great insights on the types of life work we should invest our education and experience in.

I went through my personal results during a podcast episode with Ken,[19] and it was an emotional experience for me.

I have floundered my way to a place that aligns with the three pillars. It just took me several decades to get there.

My top three talents turned out to be compassion (the ability to love on people and meet them where they are), connection (to hang out with you for five minutes is to feel like I've known you for years), and persuasion. The mission of 1000 Hours Outside combines all three of these talents, as we are sharing a message that brings hope to burdened families, connects with them in a myriad of ways in person and online, and persuades them to set their screens aside just a little bit more to partake in the full life that is right in front of them.

Ken went on with my assessment. My top passions were caregiving, performing, and advising. My love of piano performance has always been there, and these days I find myself "performing" all over the country as I teach from the stage. But it's more than just sharing information; I'm also offering care and guidance to my audience—and even to those who listen to our podcast around the world—hoping they feel supported and understood. My goal in all these situations is for those listening to laugh, cry, and leave the event or turn off the podcast episode feeling seen, encouraged, and equipped to take on their own challenges.

Finally, my top mission was service. I'm motivated by things like protecting the vulnerable. The big reveal in my assessment was the following purpose statement: "I was created to use my talents of compassion, persuasion, and connection to perform my passions of performing, caregiving, and advising, to accomplish my mission of service by producing, assistance, and protection."

This is such a far cry from the list of the half-dozen jobs I thought I might be good at in adulthood. Interestingly, twenty-five years post–high school graduation, I have found my way to a path that encompasses my purpose statement. And with this newfound clarity, I immediately set off to further my education and experience in these areas. I added books to my collection such as *Creativity, Inc.* by Ed Catmull because imagination was in my second-tier set of talents and I wanted to work on getting better at that. I started reading *Yes, And* by Kelly Leonard and Tom Yorton, which is about improvisation and how it improves creativity and collaboration.

I am thrilled to be reading these books. Additionally, I've started watching videos on improv. Maybe I'll even join a class. I already have opportunities lined up to practice because I speak around the country to large audiences.

As Ken was recommending book ideas, my soul felt like it was expanding to the point of bursting. I hadn't felt this way when I was assigned lessons in school. But this learning? Sign me up for all of it! Learning is fun. It is. But only when there is freedom attached to it. Freedom to quit, divert, expand, contract, try, do, practice, and grow.

Alfie Kohn addresses this directly in his book *Feel-Bad Education*:

> If a certain approach to teaching left most of *us* bored and unenlightened, we probably shouldn't teach another generation the same way. As far as I can tell, the vast majority of adults were themselves children at one point or another. So why do educators subject kids—and why do parents allow their kids to be subjected—to the stuff we barely found tolerable? Have we forgotten what it was like? Or do we, for lack of empathy, regard the lectures, worksheets, tests, grades and homework as a rite of passage?[20]

I recently spoke to a mom who requires her older teens to talk with twelve to fifteen adults who are in different walks of life and ask them, "What advice would you give to an eighteen-year-old? Would it be okay to meet and learn from you?"

Another mom of teens told me she wants her high schoolers to "do things." Do as many things as they can. Work with a cousin and learn how to tile bathrooms, volunteer for a CSA, work at a summer camp, etc. This may be one of the only times in life when they can work for free while gaining valuable knowledge about themselves and the world.

In all of this, there is freedom. Homeschooling allows kids the opportunities to try things, all sorts of things, from early childhood on. When societal fears, expectations, and restrictions enter the picture, they dampen a child's ability to initiate and execute their own ideas, which are crucial for creative and cognitive growth.

In an era marked by considerable stress, rapid changes, and the troubling trend of reducing recess in schools, play continues to be a lifeline for children. When we provide children of all ages the space and time to engage in meaningful play, we are giving them not only what is fun and life-giving but also what is needed. Play restores our joy and vitality. Because children innately know what they need for their own growth and development, play is not just recreation but a fundamental aspect of their childhoods. Encouraging children to engage in play, particularly with a multi-age group, is not just beneficial but essential. It helps them practice courage and develop interpersonal skills, and when you take this freedom outside, it helps boost kids' immune systems.

But freedom through homeschooling is about much more than just self-structured play—it's about giving our children the time, space, and trust to explore their world at their own pace. By stepping back from the pressures of structured activities and scheduled programs, we allow our children to develop their own interests, build self-reliance, and experience the joy of spontaneous discovery. This freedom fosters creativity, resilience, and emotional well-being, laying a strong foundation for lifelong learning and happiness.

As we embrace the freedom that homeschooling provides, we can create environments that encourage exploration, independence, and self-directed learning. Whether through play, nature, or simply allowing our children to follow their curiosities, we are giving them the gift of freedom—a gift that will serve them well throughout their lives. By prioritizing freedom, we are truly doing homeschooling right, ensuring that our children grow up with the skills, confidence, and happiness they need to thrive.

# 8

# You Are Slowing Down

It's not just what you make of your time, it's whether you have the time to make it your own.

—Kim John Payne, *Simplicity Parenting*[1]

In a world that constantly urges us to hurry, the gift of homeschooling is the ability to slow down. John Holt wrote in *Learning All the Time*, "Real learning is a process of discovery, and if we want it to happen, we must create the kind of conditions in which discoveries are made. We know what these are. They include time, leisure, freedom and lack of pressure."[2] These elements are often missing in traditional schooling. In contrast, homeschooling provides the spaciousness children need to discover and learn naturally.

These three sentences from John have always been thought-provoking to me. He states clearly that we all know that lack of pressure and a feeling or freedom and leisure precede learning. Alfie Kohn goes down a similar path in his book *Feel-Bad Education*, in the introduction chapter called "Well, Duh!: Obvious Truths That We Shouldn't Be Ignoring."

I have grappled with John's definitive statement, but I gather that we do know, even if we haven't thought about it much. As I write this book, we are muddling our way through enhancing our podcast setup. *The 1000 Hours Outside Podcast*, as of writing this, has been going for about three years, with nine million downloads. By the time you read this book, it'll likely be over ten million downloads. I just recently switched to a real microphone setup that I thought was going to solve everything but has left some words sounding a little jumbled. Every time I go to edit an episode, I'm reminded that I need to figure this out. I need to learn what's going on, why it's happening, and how to fix it. I need time, leisure, freedom, and lack of pressure.

The conditions that John says are needed to make discoveries and really learn do not make me think of government schooling at all. In fact, quite the opposite. Most would say that school is not filled with open swaths of time but rather regimented smaller blocks of time divided up by bells, transitions, and teacher instruction.

These days, as recess times have continued to be cut short, there is rarely enough free time that is solely for enjoyment during the school day. Voice of Play wrote an article in 2018, using survey results from the International Play Equipment Manufacturers Association (IPEMA) showing that "of the teachers surveyed, 93 percent said that their school currently offers recess for its students, and the average length is 25 minutes per day."[3] Twenty-five minutes. Where we live, kids in traditional school settings are out of the home for close to nine hours a day. It takes some kids longer than others to get to and from school, but even if the school day took up just six hours of their day, recess accounts for only 7%

of that time. That is all we are giving to children for their leisure—7%.

This is happening even though teachers are well aware of the positive impact of recess. The survey results from IPEMA showed that 97% of teachers noted that recess improved the conduct of students who tend to behave poorly, and 95% of teachers agreed that students' social interactions improved when they played together outside.[4] Even so, there are other forces beyond the teachers' control that influence these decisions about length of recess. Ample time to play is not a given for children who are enrolled in the public education system.

## Time, Leisure, Freedom, and Lack of Pressure

Angela Hanscom observed a troubling trend in her clinical practice. The traditional, brightly colored indoor therapy spaces, replete with swings and ball pits, often left children in a state of sensory overload. But when she took kids outside to feel the actual wind instead of blowing a fan in their faces, it provided the sensory richness they needed, without the overwhelm.

Therapeutic settings often limit natural, vigorous play. It dawned on Angela that these man-made environments might have been stifling rather than aiding the very sensory and motor development they were intended to support. These observations led to a pivotal shift in her career: from indoor clinics to the great outdoors, where she founded Timber-Nook—an innovative program that immerses children in nature, encouraging them to explore, take risks, and simply play.

When she first started running TimberNook, a program she originally thought would run for only one summer, she told me she was the entertainer. That first summer, the staff tried a model of acting out children's stories in the woods. For example, they set out bricks, sticks, and straw bales, giving the kids the opportunity to reenact "The Three Little Pigs."

But after that summer, once Angela realized the demand was so great that she would continue the program, she shifted her approach. "I was really entertaining them," she told me. "I had an adult-directed activity outside for them every thirty to forty-five minutes." TimberNook shifted from this model to be more experimental and experiential for the children. The adults would stage an environment that inspired play, but then, instead of directing from one activity to the next, they would "kind of fade into the backdrop and allow the kids to take the lead."[5]

You may recall that I spoke of Joelle Hanscom, Angela's daughter, earlier in this book. Joelle told me tales about her childhood that were drenched in nature. As a high school senior, Joelle spoke eloquently of the benefits that she believes she received through all that leisure time in the woods. The conversation painted a picture of outdoor play as the cornerstone of her childhood. Having time of her own deeply influenced her personal development and values.

For Joelle, the natural world was not just a backdrop but a vibrant, interactive space that nurtured her independence and resilience. She recalls how the freedom to explore, to climb trees, and to navigate streams allowed her to develop a keen sense of risk assessment and self-reliance. This kind of play—largely unmediated by adult supervision as her mom and other staff learned to step back—taught her critical problem-solving skills and confidence, attributes she will carry into her adult life.

As Joelle has gotten older, she has been able to contrast her own childhood with what she observes in her peers, many of whom were raised in digitally saturated environments, as is often the case these days. Some of the biggest differences she notes are in bravery, initiative, social skills, and identity.

Joelle regaled me with thrilling tales of daring adventures in the woods, attributing her ability to face other challenges head-on to the countless hours she spent engaging with the natural environment. Even without being told what to do, where to go, or how to spend her time, she learned to push her limits and embrace the unknown. This bravery, she explained, extended beyond the physical, outdoor play to eventually influence her academic and personal decisions. "Bravery," she told me, "goes a long way in life. Most kids that didn't have an outdoor childhood aren't as brave."

Each summer, the kids at TimberNook would create make-believe societies. The camp was set deep in the woods, where thick canopies of leaves filtered the sunlight into warm, cozy patches. The forest floor became the canvas for Joelle and her TimberNook friends to create their own society each year, marked by elaborate games that blurred the lines between reality and imagination. They designated roles that felt as real to them as any job. Their intricate society involved daily missions that employed spies weaving through the underbrush, messengers darting between tree trunks, and treasure keepers guarding their hoards of pine cones and shiny, smooth stones that were deemed precious gems. The economy of the woods spurred their imagination and delight. "A pine cone was like a dollar bill," Joelle told me, but "you were rich if you had gems."

Joelle reminisced about constructing forts from fallen branches and large leaves, crafting structures that stood as proud testaments to the kids' creativity and teamwork. These weren't just haphazard piles of wood; they were castles and fortresses, meticulously designed with entrances masked by ferns and moss. The children learned to use tarps to preserve their creations and protect them from the elements. They divided themselves into tribes, boys against girls, with each fort a bastion in their playful wars, where strategies were whispered under the rustle of leaves and laughter echoed through the trees.

All this communal, free-spirited play wasn't just for fun; it was foundational for developing communication skills and an ability to engage on a deeper level with others. As Joelle stated earlier, she can hold a conversation with a person that lasts longer than a minute. She is proud of that, as she should be.

These days, kids are not afforded time to come up with their own play experiences. A twenty-five-minute recess simply isn't enough time. Angela often reminds those she speaks to that it can take up to forty-five minutes for children to develop a play scheme, and longer if they aren't used to playing. Every school day, all across the United States, recess ends before children even have the chance to fall into it, to become deeply absorbed in their imaginations. But homeschooling equals time. It encompasses all the conditions John Holt outlines: freedom, leisure, time, and lack of pressure—the very same conditions that Joelle attributes to helping her develop bravery, a sense of identity, and so much more. "While most kids my age struggle with their identities, I know exactly who I am." She added, "People appreciate when you're yourself."[6]

## Becoming Enduringly Popular

Kim John Payne echoed much of what Joelle was experiencing when he told me, "Low-screen and no-screen kids are enduringly popular, not intermittently popular."[7]

In days gone by, kids had more time to call their own. I talk about these cultural shifts in the United States and across much of the developed world in my book *Until the Streetlights Come On.* As recess has waned while homework, extracurricular activities, and screen usage have skyrocketed, we are left with lost children. We have stolen their time.

School lunchrooms and hallways look and sound much different from when we were kids. Today, kids report that phones come out before lessons start and again as soon as lessons are over. Joelle observed, "Everyone is constantly looking at their phones and typing." Sean Killingsworth, founder of The Reconnect Movement, reported much of the same. "Kids would try and go on their phone secretly in class instead of trying to talk to each other."[8]

Honest conversations with iGen (the internet generation), a term coined by Jean Twenge, are gut-wrenching. Sean describes his friends this way: "They're waiting for you to stop talking to them as soon as you begin talking to them."

"A childhood on the screens is not really a childhood," Joelle observes. "If kids could go back and relive their childhood without screens, they would greatly appreciate the lack of screen time because it changes your perspective on the world as well."[9]

*American Girls* by Nancy Jo Sales is the most jaw-dropping book I've read about childhood being ripped away from children. Of all the books I've read about kids and screen use, this one stirred up the most empathy in me toward the plight of kids, both guys and girls. They are in this conundrum where screens that seem so necessary for them to fit in are actually making them miserable.

"Childhood is gone," Nancy Jo writes. Gone are the days of pine cone dollars and forts made of tree limbs. We've replaced these quintessential parts of childhood with screens and social media. One teenage girl Nancy interviewed said, "I'm so happy when I get likes. We're all obsessed with how many likes we get. Everyone says, 'I get no likes,' but everyone says that even if they get likes—it never feels like enough. I feel like I'm brainwashed into wanting likes." Another said, "How you look is all anybody cares about anymore. Being beautiful nowadays is seen as way better than being smart."[10]

Not one young adult speaks of their childhood on screens the way Joelle speaks of her childhood at TimberNook.

But Sean has hope. He says, "We have the opportunity to be leaders in our generation. We have the opportunity to show other people that it's okay to interact in person authentically."[11]

Both Sean and Joelle spoke of lost authenticity. This is echoed in Nancy's book time and time again in statements such as, "All people care about now is, 'How do I look on social media?' It makes girls feel like they have to try so hard to get people to like them. . . . Some people feel bad if they don't get enough likes and comments. . . . Half the time it doesn't even look like you. . . . You're getting people to like this picture of you that isn't even real."[12]

Biologist and cofounder of 10X Health System, Gary Brecka, teaches about authenticity. In a viral video clip of him speaking at a 10X Ladies conference, he gives a brief explanation of energy and frequency. He tells the audience that for years, the concept of the law of attraction seemed like mere folklore. He dismissed it until he stumbled upon two principles in physics known as constructive interference and destructive interference. The constructive interference law posits that when two waves of identical lengths intersect, their amplitudes combine to double the original intensity. Deconstructive interference has the opposite effect and occurs when one wavelength is up while the other is down, so the two wavelengths add up to zero. They cancel each other out so that there is no wavelength left.[13]

This discovery sparked Gary's interest and led him to explore the potential of energy exchange in human conversations. "What this means is that you can get energy from conversation," Gary told his audience. "You can get energy from the people around you, or they can take energy away from you."[14]

Further exploration brought Gary to an intriguing study called the "Spane Scale of Emotion." In this extensive research involving 25,000 participants, scientists were able to measure with remarkable precision the emotional frequency emitted by individuals. They distinguished among various emotions, from anger and passion to joy and despair, based on the unique frequencies they emitted. Surprisingly, the research revealed that the strongest frequency emitted was that of authenticity—measuring at a rate 4,000 times more potent than that of love.

There is transformative power in being a genuine and authentic person because we impact not only ourselves but those around us. Learning who we are takes time and requires stepping away from the kind of pressure that Nancy

Jo describes: "Some girls wanted attention so bad, it was like they would do anything for it. Anything for the likes."[15]

The ramifications of a shortage of time, leisure, freedom, and lack of pressure become apparent in time. Kim John Payne described kids who could talk only about TikTok or whatever they've seen on the screen. I've been privy to some of those conversations. I once had dinner with a family whose teens talked only about TikTok for the entire conversation. Who was following who? Who wasn't following who? Who posted this? Did you see that? Screen talk dominated the dinner.

While low-screen or no-screen kids may be on the "periphery of those fluff conversations," as Kim says, they can get to the core of a conversation when it turns to something more meaningful.

When you are slowing down in your home by setting aside loads of seatwork, screens, and a litany of after-school special programs, remember that you are nurturing a lifestyle that promotes authenticity and self-expression. As Kim put it, "Consider the differences between high visibility, intermittent popularity and low-key, enduring popularity. We do not want to sacrifice our kids' precious sense of self in order for them to become the cool kids of the moment."[16]

## Shouldn't We Be Speeding Up?

We are living in an era marked by unprecedented technological advancement. Generative artificial intelligence (GAI) is one of the most transformative forces of our time. Though our computers look relatively similar to how they did in the 1980s and 1990s (albeit more streamlined and lighter weight), the technology driving the computers has changed dramatically. Ryan Collins, author of *The God of Tech*, calls artificial intelligence "the science of making computers think like humans."[17]

The conversation around AI moved from theoretical discussions to practical implications before many of us even knew exactly what it was. I interviewed Jerry Kaplan about his book *Generative Artificial Intelligence: What Everybody Needs to Know* and aired the interview the week his book launched into the world.[18] Though I had heard of AI, I had not yet heard of GAI. It turns out I wasn't alone. When we published the podcast episode, I took an informal poll. The results were quite surprising. Only 18% of the participants had heard of GAI, while 81% were hearing of it for the very first time. When I told Jerry, he was astonished. GAI is affecting everything from job markets to personal relationships, and yet many parents are unaware of the scope.

Ben Angel is a bestselling author who has predicted business, health, and tech trends for nearly twenty years. As he told me in a podcast episode, "We have a small window where public opinion can influence the unfolding of AI, but this window is rapidly closing."[19] This sentiment captures the urgency to engage with and understand AI—not just as passive observers but as active participants shaping its integration into society.

Fast-moving technologies and swift changes produce an undercurrent of rush among people. We loathe the idea of being left behind, and yet we must come to grips with the fact that we will be. Ryan Collins teaches a bit about quantum computing, which "allows for an exponentially faster, more-optimized way to store, transport, and compute data than classical computing. The data that would take today's fastest classical supercomputers years to process, will take a quantum computer seconds or minutes."[20]

And just for fun, quantum computers use qubits instead of bits. A qubit (also called a quantum bit) is the basic unit of information in a quantum computer. In classical computing, a regular bit can be either a 0 or a 1, but a qubit can exist in a state of 0, 1, or both at the same time. This ability to hold multiple states, which is called "superposition," simultaneously allows quantum computers to process information much more efficiently for certain tasks. "The quantum state of qubits in superposition and entanglement is extremely sensitive," Collins writes. "The smallest disturbance or 'noise,' such as a vibration or a slight change in temperature, can cause the quantum state to disappear. This is called decoherence. Scientists and researchers do their best to reduce noise by housing qubits in supercooled fridges at temperatures colder than deep space."[21]

Is your head spinning yet? Maybe you're just learning about GAI for the first time, and now you've learned that there are temperatures colder than deep space. Just how cold is that?

Quantum computers and these marvelous qubits are already here! Ryan gives us the stats. In 2021, IBM built a 127-qubit quantum computer. By 2022, they'd managed 433 qubits, and the goal is 4,000 qubits by 2025.[22]

This shift brings a mix of excitement, confusion, and apprehension, particularly among parents concerned about the world their children will inherit. The pace is both exhilarating and daunting. For today's kids, AI is not a distant reality but a present tool. From educational aids to virtual companions, the application of AI in the lives of kids has already arrived. Children must learn how to navigate a world where AI-generated content blends seamlessly with human-created information.

So what should our response to all this be as parents? Fear could lead us to "double down on old ways," as psychologist and author Madeline Levine says.[23] "It's so difficult for parents to reconsider the metrics that served them well in their own formative years—test scores, college admissions, that degree from Brown." Why? Because "last century did not demand lifelong, continuous adaptation to a swiftly evolving environment."[24]

Times have changed. This means the metrics of success have changed as well.

What then shall we do? Run faster? Chase more? More tutors, more study, more extracurriculars? No. Remember that these represent the metrics of a time that no longer exists.

What will the future hold? We have some good news here.

The future will still hold jobs. Jobs will not become obsolete or be completely taken over by artificial intelligence. Technological advancements increase wealth, and though the job market will change, there will still be jobs. Jerry Kaplan explains it in this somewhat counterintuitive way:

> We've automated nearly 98 percent of all work people did in 1800, and yet, here we are at full employment, with lots of employers unable to find enough workers. Clearly, automation puts people out of work. That's the whole point—it substitutes capital for labor. And yet after each previous wave of automation, the number of jobs has increased. What's going on? The answer is that somehow, our rising expectations

and standard of living seem to magically keep pace with our available time and wealth, which generates new jobs.[25]

I found this to be one of the most entertaining and thought-provoking lines of Jerry's book *Generative Artificial Intelligence*: "Imagine what the average person from 1800 would think if they could see us today. They would think we have all gone crazy. Why not work a few hours a week, buy a sack of potatoes and a jug of wine, build a shack in the woods, dig a hole for an outhouse, and live a life of leisure?"[26]

Humans innately desire more and better. Though a sack of potatoes and a shack might be sufficient, as our means grow, we almost universally enhance our situations and surroundings. All that said, AI's impact on the job market is profound. Automation always leads to initial job losses, and this wave of generative AI is causing cognitive automation. In other words, certain jobs that were never at risk in the past may be at risk in the future. Google's reported reduction of 30,000 jobs due to AI advancements is an example of a trend in which AI targets certain cognitive tasks with marked efficiency and undermines many types of roles; even some that require high levels of education and skill are not exempt.

For parents, the economic implications are a source of anxiety. The fear is not just about job displacement but the broader economic stability of their households.

But let's not double down on the old ways. Instead, let's pull back. Do less. Play more. As AI transforms industries, the ability to pivot and adapt becomes crucial. The skills that children (and parents) need in this wave of automation include adaptability, problem-solving, and critical thinking since navigating multiple career shifts will be the norm for most.

Pause and consider your own life. Did studying and taking tests help you become the type of person who is adaptable enough to make multiple career shifts? Did nightly homework assignments enhance your critical thinking? Or did those skills come through time on your own, when you were able to engage with and wrestle with life's questions?

In April 2024, we were packing up our family and our business merchandise (as we often do in the spring months) to speak at a homeschooling and parenting convention in Pigeon Forge, Tennessee. The day before we were set to leave was an unusually warm spring day in Michigan, so we took full advantage of it and spent the afternoon at the beach. The day rolled away from us, as the days sometimes do, and I found myself wrapping up a podcast edit at 1:00 in the morning and I still hadn't packed. We were going to be away from home for six days—three days at the conference in Pigeon Forge and three days in the Nashville area, where we were meeting up with some friends as well as taping a few in-person podcasts at the Dave Ramsey headquarters. There was a lot to think through, and we had to be on the road early to make it to our 4:00 p.m. setup time in Tennessee. The drive south from Michigan was a little over eight hours, so we had to leave at or before dawn. I figured I would get a little shut-eye, get up early, try to pack as best I could, and hopefully catch a little catnap during the drive.

Somewhere around 2:45 a.m., my plans began to shift because a visitor joined me in our room. At first, it appeared to be a nightmare. Some figure with long, dark hair was grabbing at my feet. I was alarmed. Who was in our bedroom?!

My heart rate began to drop as I realized it was our seven-year-old daughter, who came to inform me that she had a rock in her eye. Though I knew she didn't actually have a rock in her eye, it was plausible she had a piece of sand in there since we had spent our day making sandcastles at the beach. We took some time to let our eyes adjust to the bathroom lights and then went about employing all manner of ideas to remove said rock. We did the water-splash method, hot washcloth compress, eye drops, and the like—all to no avail. In a last-ditch effort to try to return to my bed, I smeared some coconut oil on her face, and it was the miraculous cure.

At this point, I knew there was no way I would be able to thoroughly pack on such little sleep, so at the last minute, I decided that my daughter and I would drive separately, leaving the booth setup to the rest of the family. And in that middle-of-the-night moment, I loathed what our family was doing. These conferences felt too hard, too complicated. There were too many moving pieces. I vowed to myself to quit.

The morning came, and we took it slow, just the two of us. I had time to pack without feeling rushed. We got on the road when we were ready, and the drive included elation (listening to audiobooks and singing songs together) and tears (every time we came to a dead stop in traffic), until we finally rolled into our hotel right around midnight. The remaining six days were dreamy—a mix of in-person experiences at the conference, with friends in the area, and at the Dave Ramsey headquarters. We went to a live pirate dinner show and grabbed some cinnamon bread at Dollywood. We swam in the hotel pool; sold our incredible backpacks that come with built-in, high-visibility rain flies; taught workshops; and talked to person after person who said the 1000 Hours Outside movement changed their lives.

It's these types of ordinary occurrences that require a little grit and fortitude, that help me learn adaptability, problem-solving, and critical thinking. As it turns out, it was nice to have two vehicles at the convention. It allowed us to adventure a little bit more, to do a little bit more with friends.

The ability to pivot comes in the doing, and we can only do new and challenging things when we have time to try new things.

## The Human Touch

The great news is that it's in the margins of your day that kids learn the skills they will need to navigate rapid changes in the job market. Dr. Carla Hannaford says, "The most important activity we can engage in to increase brain integration is unstructured, imaginative play."[27] Brain integration involves strengthening the connections between the left and right hemispheres of the brain.

Jerry Kaplan radiates optimism when he discusses his view on the evolving job landscape. He shares an excitement about possible jobs of the future that will "involve person-to-person communication skills, the ability to understand or sympathize with another person, or the authentic expression of human emotion." In an increasingly technological world, we will have an even greater need for humanness. "In the future, the attention of a human being will be more highly valued than it is today, not less."[28]

We are not in the business of speeding up to try to match the pace of exponential technological growth. We can't. Instead, we are tasked with seeking out what makes us uniquely human and provides the world with the human touch. All of this takes time. Kim John Payne says, "Emotional intelligence cannot be rushed."[29] Sherry Turkle, author of *Reclaiming Conversation*, reminds us that "most conversations take at least seven minutes to really begin."[30] Our incessant use of technology is a way to escape uncomfortable feelings of awkwardness in the moment, but to the detriment of our interpersonal skills.

More than ever, kids need time of their own. They need to direct their own play. They need stories. They need conversations. I love how Sarah Mackenzie, founder of Read-Aloud Revival, puts it: "We do have the tendency to overcomplicate things."[31]

As we slow down through our homeschooling lifestyle, our kids naturally gain more freedom, and this teaches us as parents to trust them more, all while the kids are learning a foundational trust in themselves. Joelle Hanscom wisely asserts, "Adults can best help kids by being in the background. You can do more by stepping back."[32]

Trying to keep up will never work. We must purposefully choose to slow down, to watch the clouds go by and listen to the birds sing. To read novels of daring adventure and make messes in the kitchen. It takes a long time for us to become who we are, and homeschooling gives all of us, parents included, the time to do so.

# 9

# You Are Safeguarding

A prudent man sees the evil and hides himself, but the simple
pass on and are punished [with suffering].

Proverbs 27:12 AMPC

Homeschooling offers a unique opportunity to protect our
children from the myriad challenges they might face in traditional school environments. One of the most significant
threats is bullying, a pervasive issue that can leave lasting
scars on a child's emotional and psychological well-being.
My conversations with Kim John Payne, a renowned counselor and educator, have deeply influenced my understanding
of how to navigate these challenges. His book *Emotionally
Resilient Tweens and Teens* provides invaluable insights and
practical strategies that have proven indispensable in our
journey as a homeschooling family. I was beyond impressed
at his knack for using printed words to connect with parents in a way that shows us we have what it takes to help
our children if and when they find themselves in a situation
where they are being bullied, teased, or socially excluded.

When I read Kim's book to prepare for a podcast interview, I found the information fascinating and even helpful for myself as an adult, though we had no need for it in regard to our children at the time. But as is often the case in parenting, that changed overnight. And in some dark moments when we weren't sure what to do as a result of significant and incessant bullying that one of our children was experiencing—at church, of all places—we turned to many of the principles in *Emotionally Resilient Tweens and Teens* to help carry our kids and our family through.

## The Reality of Bullying

As I travel the country to speak to homeschool parents and prospective homeschool parents, so many desperate moms and dads who are frantically searching for answers share tales of bullying. These are parents of kids of all ages.

A quick search online leads to story after story of children who have been relentlessly bullied and then ended up being homeschooled. It's important to know that the chance of being mistreated by other children is higher in both public and private school settings than in homeschool settings. Dewey Cornell, an education professor at the University of Virginia and an expert on bullying, explains, "Bullying is a ubiquitous social problem seen in nearly all schools, public or private." He goes on to say that bullying can even play a part in student shootings and suicide. "Private schools . . . have no immunity from these outcomes."[1]

Often, as a society, we attempt to downplay bullying. We say things like the old adage "Sticks and stones may break my bones, but words will never hurt me." Yet I can still remember when a classmate in the sixth grade asked me if my mom still dressed me and when I was teased regularly throughout elementary and middle school regarding my weight. I'm sure that throughout those years, positive things were said to me too—probably many positive things. But our brains are wired to remember the negative. This is called negativity bias. Professional photographer, creative director, and filmmaker Joy Prouty explains it like this: "The brain is like Velcro for negative experiences, but Teflon for positive ones." She explains some of the research behind negativity bias: "A negative experience takes only *one second* to imprint the memory upon the brain, while a positive experience takes *twenty to thirty seconds* to imprint."[2]

This might explain our memories as they stand. Basically, we immediately remember any bullying experience, but it would take twenty to thirty seconds of compliments for them to stick. I have rarely in my own life had lavish praise bestowed upon me for half a minute straight, though after learning this I've reconsidered how I encourage others. It simply needs to be longer in order to stick. Once, someone came up to me after an event I was speaking at and exclaimed, "You're the comedian!" (which I wasn't technically; I was just another speaker, but I'll take it!). He went on, "I loved your set from top to bottom. Every story that you told was relatable." That stuck. I also wrote it down immediately, so that might also be why it stuck. Either way, I'm increasing my support and praise of others to several sentences instead of one and have become more aware of just how damaging bullying can be because we are so prone to internalize it.

Some might argue that experiencing bullying is a rite of passage or something we have to learn about in order to

185

be prepared for adulthood, yet there are millions of home-schoolers who are successful adults without having experienced the lingering effects of bullying. The tricky thing about bullying is that unless you have experienced it yourself, there is no way to fully understand the depths of it. Amy Blevins, creator of the blog *Ben and Me*, writes, "Unless you've been bullied yourself and know exactly how it feels—don't ever say it's not a big deal. You don't know. It doesn't always make you stronger; sometimes it breaks you. Permanently. I'm not just talking about suicide either. I'm also talking about a lifetime of dealing with panic attacks, PTSD, and other mental and emotional scars."[3]

Dr. Phil has long spoken out against the harmful effects of bullying. In a *Dr. Phil* episode from October 2022, he discussed the extent of the current state of bullying behaviors. "Bullying does not just take place in the schoolyard anymore. Teens, tweens, and even younger kids are being bullied, taunted, shamed, and humiliated from every angle because, with the internet and the prevalence of social media, there are always ways to target a victim—oftentimes anonymously."[4] He advises: Stand with and protect your child.

Stephen Miller tells stories of his childhood in his book *The Art of Getting It Wrong*.[5] Through his writing, he conveys the depth of complexities that arise from harsh treatment by peers during childhood and the long-lasting impacts that resonate well into adulthood. Now in his forties, Miller vividly recalls the harsh realities of his childhood bullying—how it wasn't just an isolated series of incidents but had a profound influence on his self-image, interpersonal relationships, and coping mechanisms far beyond his schooling years.

Miller grew up in challenging circumstances—poverty and familial instability were the backdrops of his early life. But it was the relentless bullying he endured that left an indelible mark. He was the obese kid in school, subjected to ridicule for his weight and high-pitched voice, which didn't deepen until late in his high school years. The bullying wasn't just verbal; it involved physical attacks, like being pelted with rocks and punched. These experiences were not only physically painful but deeply humiliating, contributing to a long-term impact on his self-esteem.

The defense mechanisms Miller developed in response to these attacks were telling. He honed a sharp wit and a biting sense of humor as shields against the cruelty of his peers. Yet these tools, while protective in the moment, also had their downsides in the long run. They sometimes alienated others and could be perceived as harsh, impacting his relationships even as an adult because this reflexive sarcasm—a direct result of his need to protect himself from emotional pain—remained a part of his interactions even after high school graduation.

Miller's narrative about himself in adulthood continues to be influenced by the bullying he endured. When he looks in the mirror, especially in moments of vulnerability like at the gym or while eating, he frequently hears echoes of the derogatory terms he was called in childhood. This internal dialogue shows how deeply bullying can ingrain negative self-perceptions, which can persist despite a person's achievements or changes in their external circumstances.

Moreover, Miller's approach to parenting and self-improvement is heavily colored by his past. His determination to prove himself—to be the best at his various endeavors, whether in his YouTube presence, in real estate, or as a parent—is fueled by an underlying drive to counteract the narrative of inadequacy that bullying instilled in him. This compulsive striving for success and validation can be seen as a direct response to his experiences of being demeaned and undervalued as a child.

Miller's story is a powerful example of how the scars of bullying do not simply fade with time or success. They shape the lens through which people view themselves, often across a lifetime.

## When Schools Fall Short on Bullying

Current statistics say 20% of kids report being bullied at school, and yet, according to the same study, "Only 46% of bullied students report notifying an adult at school about the incident."[6] So it's likely that the actual numbers are higher. According to a report from the Centers for Disease Control and Prevention in 2019, "Students who experience bullying are at increased risk for depression, anxiety, sleep difficulties, lower academic achievement, and dropping out of school."[7]

Are being raised and taught at home as a form of protection helping or hindering children? Considering the lifelong impact bullying often has, in combination with how often the problem eludes comprehensive institutional solutions, a child is safer psychologically at home (except in extreme circumstances).

Kim John Payne, drawing from his extensive experience as a counselor and educator, reiterates the very real limitations that are inherent within school systems when tackling issues like bullying and social exclusion. This is a multilayered, complex problem because the dynamics of bullying are often deeply embedded in social interactions that can be obscure and resistant to straightforward interventions.

Kim's insights reveal that there is a crucial gap in schools' ability to fully grasp or intervene effectively in the nuanced social dynamics that underpin bullying. He points out that while schools may make efforts to stop bullying, these are often inconsistent and vary significantly from one educator to another. Interventions often take too long to implement, and when they fail to address the root causes and dynamics of bullying, the behaviors are only suspended temporarily or pushed further out of the sight of the grown-ups.

Additionally, Kim explains the ineffectiveness of traditional punitive measures, which paradoxically mimic the very behaviors they intend to eradicate, such as using authority to "bully the bully." This approach not only fails to address the underlying issues but also models inappropriate responses to conflict.

## Strengthening the Family Base Camp

Kim does have answers for the family, answers that our own family has used successfully. His deceptively simple premise is "strengthening the family base camp."[8] Kim often uses insightful metaphors to illustrate his points and make the concepts more memorable. The family base camp concept is no different. It is a reminder that family plays a crucial role in nurturing stability, a sense of security, and emotional resilience in children. Base camps that are used by mountaineers offer rest, rejuvenation, and a means of preparation for facing the harsh, external challenges of the world.

Personal empowerment and resilience training are at the core of Kim's strategy. By equipping children with the emotional and social tools to understand and respond to bullying on their own terms, parents can take a more individualized and empowering approach. This method not only addresses the immediate impacts of bullying but also fosters long-term resilience and self-efficacy, preparing children to navigate complex social environments throughout their lives.

Kim explains that the family base camp acts as a safe harbor that provides emotional support and a sense of belonging when kids might be navigating challenging social dynamics outside of the home, such as bullying and exclusion. This family base camp is not only a place of refuge but a place to learn and grow as parents teach kids life skills like managing emotions, resolving conflicts, and making thoughtful decisions. Sometimes role-playing is a helpful strategy to teach these skills.

The long-term benefits of strengthening the family base camp are profound and enduring. Children raised in supportive family environments typically demonstrate higher emotional intelligence, better stress-management skills, and more robust mental health. These qualities not only help them during their formative years but also equip them with the resilience to handle life's challenges as adults. In line with Kim's advocacy for whole-family solutions, homeschooling can be seen as strengthening the entire family's resilience, which sometimes is needed. The resolve of the family unit can be tested when the family experiences the loss of a loved one, the loss of a job, a move across the country, the loss of a friendship, a significant health diagnosis, or even adding a new baby. Activities that bring the family together, like shared meals, outdoor activities, and group projects, can reinforce the family as a supportive "base camp," providing a sense of belonging and security that mitigates the impacts of life's challenges that we all face at some point or another. This furthers children's skills to handle adversity as they grow.

Ideally, bullying situations arise infrequently rather than relentlessly. By opting for homeschooling, families can significantly diminish the incidence and impact of bullying on children. Homeschooling, while not an insulated bubble, exposes kids to much less mistreatment by peers than a traditional school environment does. In instances where it is needed, parents play an indispensable role in preparing their kids to face the world confidently and compassionately. They also have an easier exit strategy. If their child is being bullied at a particular co-op, dance class, youth group, or the like, it is a much more straightforward process to leave that situation than to unenroll the child from school.

Kim offers a lot of hope to kids. When we spoke, he illuminated the shortcomings of traditional school–based responses to bullying, but he also teaches parents how to empower children to advocate for themselves.

In any type of social setting that involves a bunch of kids, there are bound to be different scenarios the children will have to work through. Most often, they will navigate them with ease. In cases where bullying may arise for homeschoolers, it isn't all-encompassing. Children at home with their families experience less social turbulence. In fact, homeschooling offers a distinct advantage by significantly reducing a child's exposure to the traditional bullying hot spots found in many schools. They are not shielded from it all, but the at-home environment allows for a personalized education experience that prioritizes the child's emotional and intellectual needs. In a homeschool setting, parents can create a safe learning atmosphere where children are less likely to face the social challenges of teasing, bullying, and exclusion that are common in larger school settings. Enduring persistent bullying does not earn a child a badge of honor.

## Protecting Kids from Being Rushed

Kim has so many resources for families that we've found helpful. In *The Soul of Discipline*, he says, "Kids are exposed to too much and forced to grow up too quickly. As a result, disorientation and heightened anxiety have become the new normal."[9] Furthermore, play for a young child and downtime for a tween or teenager are critical to healthy emotional and social development.

Kim's words highlight an important aspect of homeschooling: the unique opportunity it provides parents to protect their children from the harried and often overwhelming pace of traditional school environments. This protection is not just from a physical standpoint but also from an emotional and intellectual one, offering a tailored learning experience that values depth over breadth and personal growth over conformity.

Traditional school systems have increasingly rigid schedules and curriculum demands. Not only is there little room for flexibility to chase passions, but the curriculum can inadvertently push children into a relentless race for achievement. This often leads to excessive stress and anxiety among students who struggle to keep up or who do not fit into the conventional educational molds.

Alfie Kohn warns against the dangers of comparison in his book *No Contest: The Case Against Competition.* He pulls no punches. "Competing drags us down, devastates us psychologically, poisons our relationships, interferes with our performance."[10] Moreover, he writes, "The more closely I have examined the topic, the more firmly I have become convinced that competition is an inherently undesirable arrangement, that the phrase *healthy competition* is actually a contradiction in terms."[11]

In contrast, homeschooling allows parents to set a pace that is individual and appropriate for their child's unique developmental needs, interests, and learning approach. The homeschooling lifestyle protects children by giving them the space to learn without being rushed. In a home education setting, there is no bell that signals the end of an intellectual exploration and no need to drop a subject or question because the timetable says so. This flexibility enables children to dive deeper into subjects they are passionate about, enhancing their understanding and appreciation of the material.

Each summer, our family is fascinated by monarch butterflies. We are often on the hunt for caterpillar eggs or tiny caterpillars that can be found on the underside of milkweed leaves. Homeschooling allows us the luxury of spending weeks (or sometimes an entire summer) exploring entomology, life cycles, and even the art of scientific drawing, turning what might have been a fleeting interest in a traditional classroom into a profound learning experience that is cross-curricular and cohesive.

Only when we are unhurried can we nurture a genuine love for learning. Children are more likely to retain information and develop a lifelong enthusiasm for education when they do not feel pressured to learn at an arbitrary pace. Home-school cultivates an academic environment where the question "why" is just as important as "what." This not only enhances cognitive skills but also fosters critical thinking—a skill that, as we have already seen, is indispensable in this rapidly changing world.

Additionally, homeschooling can shield children from the overwhelming competition and comparison that often characterize traditional school settings. Without the constant pressure to compete against peers for grades, rankings, or even teacher approval, children can focus on their inner selves. I love the simple question "What is something you would like to learn about today?"

I certainly can answer that question. I would like to learn from the stack of books I have waiting for me once I'm finished with this manuscript. One of them is called *Swimming to Antarctica: Tales of a Long-Distance Swimmer* by Lynne Cox. I was introduced to the genre of adventure biographies and autobiographies by Alastair Humphreys, a National Geographic Explorer of the Year. Alastair and I have spoken several times, and though we live across an ocean from each other, I always enjoy our virtual meetings. Alastair sits in front of shelves and shelves lined with books, many of which tell harrowing tales of adventure.

This is a classic example of Austin Kleon's approach of learning about the people who have influenced those who influence you. Alastair has had a huge influence on me, particularly with his concept of microadventures, in which he touts that "some adventure is better than none at all."[12] As our kids have gotten older, I have bemoaned the shifts in our calendar from those wide-open days of the baby and toddler years to the slightly more harried days of the tween and teen years. There are definitely adventures I hadn't previously considered given our limitations, but we changed our perspective after talking with Alastair.

Now we'll head to the beach when it's already near sunset to look for shark teeth for an hour or less simply because that is all the time we have, whereas before I wouldn't have considered it worth the effort. But I learned through experience that unequivocally we are always better for having said yes, even when circumstances aren't ideal.

Alastair has written many books, but two favorites of our family are *Great Adventurers: The Incredible Expeditions of 20 Explorers* and *Against the Odds: The Incredible Struggles of 20 Great Adventurers*. These books give insight into why Alastair's bookshelves are so full. In *Great Adventurers*, he introduces us to the feats of some of his personal adventure heroes. These are the men and women who have inspired him because, as he says, "I have met many people who have regretted *not* going on an adventure in their life, but I have *never* met someone who was sorry that they did."[13]

Through this book that makes a phenomenal coffee-table book (they both do!), our family learned about adventurers like Laurie Lee, who walked across Spain using his violin skills to earn money. From there we read Laurie Lee's *As I Walked Out One Midsummer Morning*. And what a read it is: "As I lay there listening, with the sun filtering across me, I thought this was how it should always be. To be charmed from sleep by a voice like this, eased softly back into life, rather than by the customary brutalities of shouts, knocking, and alarm-bells like blows on the head. The borders of consciousness are anxious enough, raw and desperate places;

we shouldn't be dragged across them like struggling thieves as if sleep was a felony."[14]

What a rabbit hole of learning, and all at our own pace!

Alastair's book *Against the Odds* focuses on overcoming struggles. Before reading the book, we'd hardly heard of any of these adventurers, reminding us that there is so much to learn about out in the world. The cartoon illustrations of mountaineer Göran Kropp are so entertaining. There are eight different scenes showing Kropp cycling from his home in Sweden to Mount Everest, pulling a trailer behind him, carrying all his climbing gear. In one of the scenes, Kropp has turned into a full-fledged snowman. In another, he is being swarmed by bugs.

Here is where this book differs from so many others. Kropp never made it to the summit of Mount Everest because a storm forced him to turn back. We learned so much about him from Alastair's book but then dug deeper in *Ultimate High: My Everest Odyssey* by Göran Kropp with David Lagercrantz. This book is a reminder that "sometimes adventures, like life, don't work out as you want them to. . . . Now and again, you simply fail." But also, "success comes in many forms."[15]

Learning in a cohesive way that supports emotional well-being is a critical area where homeschool parents play a protective role in their children's lives. Dr. Carla Hannaford teaches us, "During times of new learning or stress . . . the non-dominant brain tends to radically decrease its functioning, leaving the dominant brain to carry on primary functioning."[16] While the science is complex, the bottom line is that when children are learning something new or when they are stressed, their brain isn't working optimally. Since learning new things is a critical component of childhood, the only piece here that we can attempt to influence is the stress.

Homeschool parents can help their children learn in a way that protects their emotional well-being. In traditional schools, children can be exposed to social pressures, bullying, and other stressful interactions that may affect not only their mental health but also their ability to learn. Homeschooling can mitigate these risks by providing a safer, more controlled environment.

Furthermore, the protective environment of homeschooling helps foster better relationships within the family. Siblings can spend more time together, and activities can involve the whole family, which strengthens bonds and provides a supportive network. These strong family ties are crucial for emotional stability and can help children develop better interpersonal skills over time.

However, it's essential to address criticisms that suggest homeschooling might excessively shelter children, potentially hindering their ability to cope with real-world challenges. While it's true that homeschooling offers a more protected environment, it does not necessarily isolate children. Many homeschool families actively engage in community groups, sports, arts, and other activities that provide varied social experiences. Also, homeschool parents can introduce their children to diverse situations and challenges at a pace they deem appropriate, thus gradually equipping them with the skills to navigate the broader world effectively.

## Protecting Kids from Market Forces and Ill-Suited Content

There are other things homeschool parents are wisely protecting their children from just by choosing to have them be at home. Susan Linn speaks boldly about the market's influence on kids. Homeschooling offers a unique protective barrier against the aggressive market forces she discusses in her book *Who's Raising the Kids?: Big Tech, Big Business, and the Lives of Children.* By minimizing kids' exposure to relentless advertising and the commodification inherent in traditional school environments, homeschooling can shield children from the hyper-commercialized culture that often prioritizes consumerism over education. In homeschool, children are not subjected to the peer pressure of having the latest gadgets or fashion, nor are they bombarded by the in-school marketing that is becoming increasingly prevalent.

Additionally, homeschooling can serve as a significant safeguard against the pervasive influence of technology that is increasingly embedded within traditional school settings. As Susan discusses, many schools integrate EdTech (short for educational technology) not just as a tool for learning but also as a platform for commercial engagement and data collection, often under the guise of enhancing education. This booming industry brought in $28.3 billion in 2019, highlighting how deeply it has penetrated educational environments. Homeschooling allows parents to control the role technology plays in education, emphasizing its use as a deliberate choice for specific learning outcomes rather than as a constant presence. This controlled exposure helps children avoid the potential overreliance on digital solutions and the privacy concerns associated with data harvesting by tech companies in educational settings. By focusing on hands-on, real-world experiences and interactions, homeschooling can foster deeper learning and critical-thinking skills, free from the commercial and distracting influences that tech in schools often brings.

Susan writes, "You're dealing with a culture dominated by multinational corporations spending billions of dollars and using seductive technologies to bypass parents and target children directly with messages designed—sometimes ingeniously—to capture their hearts and minds. And their primary purpose is not to help kids lead healthy lives or to promote positive values or even to make their lives better. It's to generate profit."[17]

When I spoke with Nancy Jo Sales, author of *American Girls*, we discussed the harsh realities of adolescent life in the age of social media.[18] Nancy Jo's work highlights the deep-seated issues that arise from the pervasive influence of social media on teenagers, particularly the intense pressure to conform to certain sexualized behaviors and appearances that are constantly glorified online. Adolescent boys and girls are frequently subjected to a digital culture that prizes superficiality and objectification, a trend that is deeply embedded in their daily interactions on platforms like Instagram and Snapchat.

Homeschooling provides a unique solution to these modern challenges. By opting out of the traditional school setting, parents can significantly reduce their children's exposure to the peer pressures that drive social media culture, which is often amplified within the school environment. This reduction in exposure is crucial during the formative teenage years, as it allows students to develop a sense of self that is less influenced by the incessant demands for likes, follows, and the approval of peers. Instead, homeschooling can foster an environment where adolescents learn to value real-world interactions and achievements over digital validation.

A homeschool setting allows parents to more effectively monitor and guide their children's tech use. Unlike traditional schools, where the integration of technology is sometimes done uncritically, homeschooling can involve a more thoughtful incorporation of digital tools that enhances learning without compromising on social and emotional development. In essence, homeschooling can act as a buffer, protecting adolescents from the digital onslaught that often leads to issues such as cyberbullying, online harassment, and the stress of constant online presence, thus promoting healthier developmental outcomes.

In this intricate tapestry of parenting, homeschooling emerges not just as an educational choice but as a profound act of protection. It is a steadfast guard against the rapid currents of societal expectations and the harsh realities of bullying, offering our children a sanctuary where they can grow at their own pace, undisturbed by the turmoil that often accompanies traditional school environments. By choosing this path, we do more than educate; we empower our children with the resilience to face life's challenges with confidence. We provide a safe harbor—a nurturing ground where the seeds of self-worth, courage, and compassion are sown deep. Here, in the warm embrace of home, our children are not shielded from the world but are given the strength to meet it on their own terms, ready to turn life's adversities into stepping stones for success.

# You Are Choosing the Best Teacher for Your Child

> The fact is that no one knows your child, or cares about him, more than you do.
>
> —Israel Wayne, *Answers for Homeschooling*[1]

My favorite homeschool cartoon depicts a homeschool class reunion. The scene shows a decorated room with balloons and a banner. There's a huge punch bowl. Each guest is wearing a name tag and holding a drink or a plate of food. There's Dad, Tom, and Sis, and the mother is there but you can only see the back of her. Tom asks, "Were the name tags necessary, Mom?"

And isn't that the point? No name tags are needed because no one cares about your child more than you do.

When I was a kid, we would always walk up to the elementary school a few days before school began to see who our teacher and classmates would be. Often, there is a lot of cajoling behind the scenes—requesting this teacher or that. But ultimately, in the public school setting, those decisions are not yours.

Homeschooling is more than an educational choice; it's a commitment to nurturing, guiding, and loving your children as they grow into well-rounded individuals. Throughout this book, we've explored the myriad ways in which homeschooling benefits both children and parents, reinforcing the idea that you are the best teacher for your child.

## You Are Protecting and Nurturing

From the very first chapter, we discussed the protective environment homeschooling provides. By shielding your children from the undue pressures and rushed pace of traditional schooling, you allow them the space to grow at their own pace. This nurturing environment fosters self-reliance and confidence, qualities that will serve your children well throughout their lives.

## You Are Providing a Personalized Education

One of the most significant advantages of homeschooling is the ability to tailor education to your child's unique needs and interests. No two children are alike, and the flexibility homeschooling offers means you can create a learning experience that truly resonates with your child. This personalized approach not only makes learning more engaging but also fosters a deep, intrinsic motivation to continue to explore and understand the world around them long after their school years have ended.

## You Are Creating a Strong Family Bond

Homeschooling isn't just about academics; it's also about strengthening family relationships. The time spent learning together, exploring new subjects, and engaging in discussions fosters a deep connection between parents and children. These shared experiences create memories and bonds that will endure long after the homeschooling years are over.

## You Are Instilling Values and Character

Education is not just about imparting knowledge; it's also about shaping character. As a homeschool parent, you have the unique opportunity to weave your family's values and morals into your child's daily learning. This consistent reinforcement of values helps develop strong, principled individuals who understand the importance of integrity, kindness, and empathy.

## You Are Encouraging Curiosity and Creativity

Homeschooling encourages children to explore their interests and passions without the constraints often found in traditional schools. By allowing your children the freedom to follow their curiosity, you foster creativity and a love for discovery. Whether it's through hands-on projects, outdoor adventures, or imaginative play, homeschooling nurtures an inquisitive mind.

## You Are Ensuring Emotional and Social Development

A common misconception about homeschooling is that it limits socialization. In reality, homeschooling provides numerous opportunities for children to interact with a diverse range of people through community activities, co-ops, sports, and other group engagements. This variety of social interactions helps children develop strong social skills and emotional intelligence in a safe and supportive environment.

## You Are Adapting to Your Child's Learning Style

Every child learns differently, and one of the strengths of homeschooling is the ability to adapt teaching methods to suit individual learning styles. Whether your child learns best through visual aids, hands-on activities, or auditory instruction, you can customize your approach to ensure they grasp concepts and retain knowledge effectively.

## You Are Nurturing a Lifelong Learner

One of the most important goals of education is to cultivate a love for learning that persists throughout life. By emphasizing critical thinking, problem-solving, and a passion for discovery, you are preparing your child to be a lifelong learner. This foundation of curiosity and adaptability is essential in a rapidly changing world.

## You Are Preparing Your Child for a Changing Future

Homeschooling equips children with the skills they need to succeed in a future that is constantly evolving. By teaching them how to learn independently, manage their time, and take responsibility for their education, you are preparing them for the challenges and opportunities that lie ahead. These skills are invaluable in higher education, the workplace, and beyond.

## You Are the Best Teacher for Your Child

The decision to homeschool is a profound testament to your dedication to and love for your children. It is a journey filled with some challenges but also immense rewards. By choosing to homeschool, you are taking an active role in shaping not just your child's education but their character, values, and future as well.

As we've explored throughout this book, the benefits of homeschooling are vast and varied. But at the heart of it all is the undeniable fact that you, as a parent, are the best teacher for your child. You know their strengths and weaknesses, their hopes and dreams. You have the passion and commitment to guide them toward achieving their fullest potential, and you are in it for the long haul.

Trust in your abilities, embrace the journey, and remember that your unique perspective and deep understanding of your child make you the ideal person to lead them through their educational adventure. Homeschooling is not just about imparting knowledge; it's about inspiring a love for learning, nurturing a strong sense of self, and building a foundation for a successful, fulfilling life.

You are doing homeschooling right because you have chosen the best teacher for your children. It's you. Hands down. No one else even comes close. Your dedication and love are the greatest gifts you can give your children.

# ACKNOWLEDGMENTS

Writing this book has been a journey, and I am deeply grateful to everyone who has been along for the ride.

First and foremost, I want to thank my family—my incredible husband, Josh, and our five wonderful children. You bring joy and laughter to our homeschooling days, and your curiosity and zest for life inspire me every single day.

To my parents, Cal and Cathy, and my in-laws, Mark and Jill, thank you for your unwavering encouragement and belief in our choice to homeschool. We do not take this for granted, as we have met so many other parents around the country who have experienced additional struggles because they do not have this wonderful gift of support. Your encouragement has been the foundation upon which we've built this beautiful life of learning and exploration.

To the incredible Baker team—Olivia, Eileen, Holly, Jessica, and Joanna—thank you for your dedication and for being a constant source of inspiration. Your hard work and friendship have made this journey so much more joyful.

Jessica, you do a job I could never even dream of doing. You are my hero! I am in awe of you and so grateful for your finessing.

To Rachel, my amazing agent, thank you for believing in this project and guiding it to fruition. Your support has been invaluable, and you are a total rock star. I love sending people your way.

Suzanne, my dear friend from FPEA, what a joy it has been to walk this homeschooling path with you. The events we've shared together are memories I will cherish forever. A special shout-out to Ethan and Natalie Grace as well!

Beautiful Beth, you shower me with unwavering support and a thoughtful presence. You are dependable and brilliant. Thank you for being not just a friend but a guiding light for years upon years. I love that we are part of each other's bucket brigade.

To Emily, my favorite synchronized swimming friend, thank you for fielding all my word-count texts. Hopefully The Council deems this book worthy. Someday we should go to Buc-ee's together. "In June, when broom an' bloom was seen."

Sarah, raising and homeschooling our kids together has been so inspiring—even for the years that we have lived farther apart. What a thrill to raise kids side by side and watch them as they start to launch into the world. You and Dustin are wonderful models for homeschool parents.

Nellie, what a friendship we have forged. Homeschooling together has been a dream come true, the high point of my entire life. Your presence has made this journey rich beyond measure. I adore your whole family. You and John are truly the most capable and hardworking people we have ever known. We are there for you whenever there is foam that needs scraped off your log-cabin walls. So-rich and ferns for life!

To those who came before me and spoke truth so boldly, thank you. You paved the way for me to stand on your shoulders, and in doing so, you changed my life in a way that will ripple down several generations.

One of the beauties of homeschooling is that it has brought us so many deep and meaningful relationships with people all over the country. I could never name them all, but I do want to give a special thank-you to Roger and Jan, Joe and Zan, Jay and Heidi, Dan and Rachel, Larry and Tanya, Carlos and Tracy, Mike and Missie, Scott and Jennifer, Kevin and Suzanne, Xander and Christine, Matthias and Keilah, Aubrey and Jen, Amber, Leslie, Greta, Elsie, Ainsley, Sally, Erin, Angie, and the author of the Starborn series.

And finally, to the 1000 Hours Outside community, thank you for being the heartbeat of this movement. No matter how you've chosen to educate your children, your passion for outdoor play, connection, and exploration has created a ripple effect that reaches far beyond what any of us could have imagined. Together we are changing lives, one hour at a time. Your enthusiasm and commitment are a constant source of encouragement, and I am endlessly grateful to be on this journey with you.

# NOTES

## Introduction

1. Madeline Levine, *Ready or Not: Preparing Our Kids to Thrive in an Uncertain and Rapidly Changing World* (Harper, 2020), 5.
2. "Michigan K–12 Standards, English Language Arts," Michigan.gov, accessed September 10, 2024, https://www.michigan.gov/-/media/Project /Websites/mde/Literacy/Content-Standards/ELA_Standards.pdf.
3. "Michigan K–12 Standards."
4. "Social Studies, Grade Level Content Expectations, Grades K–8," Michigan.gov, December 2007, https://www.michigan.gov/-/media/Project /Websites/mde/Literacy/Content-Standards/SS_Standards.pdf.
5. "K–12 Physical Education Standards," Michigan.gov, May 2017, https://www.michigan.gov/-/media/Project/Websites/mde/2019/02/22/K_12 _PE_Standards_Aug_17_ADA_compliance918.pdf.
6. "K–12 Physical Education Standards."
7. Siegfried Engelmann, Phyllis Haddox, and Elaine Bruner, *Teach Your Child to Read in 100 Easy Lessons* (Avid Reader Press, 1986).
8. "Reading Instruction Requirements for Teaching Certificates," Department of Education, accessed October 25, 2024, https://www.michigan .gov/mde/services/ed-serv/ed-cert/educator-preparation-providers/reading -instruction-requirements-for-teaching-certificates.

## Chapter 1  You Are Learning Through Living

1. John Holt, quoted in Susannah Sheffer, ed., *A Life Worth Living: Selected Letters of John Holt* (Ohio State University Press, 1990), 98.
2. John Holt, *Instead of Education: Ways to Help People Do Things Better* (Sentient Publications, 2004), 13.

3. John Taylor Gatto, "The Seven Lesson Schoolteacher," Encyclopedia .com, accessed September 11, 2024, https://www.encyclopedia.com/social -sciences/applied-and-social-sciences-magazines/seven-lesson-schoolteacher.

4. John Taylor Gatto, *Dumbing Us Down: The Hidden Curriculum of Compulsory Schooling* (New Society Publishers, 2017), 3.

5. Gatto, *Dumbing Us Down*, 3.

6. Mario Ferrari and Guilio Ferrari, *Building Robots with LEGO Mindstorms* (Syngress, 2001), 287.

7. Gatto, *Dumbing Us Down*, 7.

8. "The Future of Jobs: Employment, Skills and Workforce Strategy for the Fourth Industrial Revolution," World Economic Forum, January 18, 2016, https://www3.weforum.org/docs/WEF_Future_of_Jobs.pdf.

9. Alison Kay, "Your Child's Job Probably Doesn't Exist Yet," LinkedIn, October 20, 2016, https://www.linkedin.com/pulse/your-childs-job-probably -doesnt-exist-yet-alison-kay.

10. Gatto, *Dumbing Us Down*, 7.

11. Steven Pressfield, *The War of Art: Break Through the Blocks and Win Your Inner Creative Battles* (Black Irish Entertainment, 2002), 145.

12. Nicole Runyon, "Ask the Experts: Explaining the 9-Year Change," *Grosse Pointe News*, July 26, 2023, https://www.grossepointenews.com/articles/ask-the-experts-explaining-the-9-year-change.

13. Central Michigan Lapidary and Mineral Society, https://www.michrocks.com/.

14. Teacher Tom, "How About, First and Foremost, We Agree to Not Suck the Joy from Their Lives," *Teacher Tom* (blog), August 23, 2024, https://teachertomsblog.blogspot.com/2024/08/how-about-first-and-foremost-we -agree.html.

## Chapter 2  You Are Allowing for Individual Timelines

1. "Original Quotes and Favorite Sayings from Magda Gerber," Magda Gerber Legacy, accessed September 11, 2024, https://magdagerber.org/magda -gerber-quotes/.

2. John Holt, *Learning All the Time: How Small Children Begin to Read, Write, Count, and Investigate the World, Without Being Taught* (Da Capo Press, 1989), 35.

3. Peter Gray, *Mother Nature's Pedagogy: Biological Foundations for Children's Self-Directed Education* (Alliance for Self-Directed Education, 2020), 2.

4. Gray, *Mother Nature's Pedagogy*, 72.

5. Peter Gray, *Free to Learn: Why Unleashing the Power to Play Will Make Our Children Happier, More Self-Reliant, and Better Students for Life* (Basic Books, 2015), 116.

6. Nancy Carlsson-Paige, Geralyn Bywater McLaughlin, and Joan Wolfsheimer Almon, "Reading Instruction in Kindergarten: Little to Gain and

Much to Lose," Alliance for Childhood, January 2015, https://files.eric.ed.gov/fulltext/ED609172.pdf.

7. Derek R. Becker et al., "Behavioral Self-Regulation and Executive Function Both Predict Visuomotor Skills and Early Academic Achievement," *Science Direct* 29, no. 4 (2014), https://www.sciencedirect.com/science/article/abs/pii/S0885200614000428.

8. Holt, *Learning All the Time*, 19.

9. Ginny Yurich and Dr. Carla Hannaford, "We Must Reinsert Movement into Childhood," January 13, 2022, in *The 1000 Hours Outside Podcast*, produced by Open Air Productions, https://podcasts.apple.com/us/podcast/the-1000-hours-outside-podcast/id1448210728?i=1000547772474.

10. Justin Whitmel Earley, *Made for People: Why We Drift into Loneliness and How to Fight for a Life of Friendship* (Zondervan, 2023), 143.

11. Joy Marie Clarkson, *You Are a Tree: And Other Metaphors to Nourish Life, Thought, and Prayer* (Bethany House Publishers, 2024), 95.

## Chapter 3 You Are Leaving Space for Boredom

1. Nicholas Kardaras, *Glow Kids: How Screen Addiction Is Hijacking Our Kids—and How to Break the Trance* (St. Martin's Griffin, 2016), 127.

2. Kim John Payne, Luis Fernando Llosa, and Scott Lancaster, *Beyond Winning: Smart Parenting in a Toxic Sports Environment* (Lyons Press, 2013), 91.

3. Angela Hanscom, *Balanced and Barefoot: How Unrestricted Outdoor Play Makes for Strong, Confident, and Capable Children* (New Harbinger Publications, 2016), 123.

4. Glennon Doyle, *Untamed* (The Dial Press, 2020), 158.

5. "Charity (Tzedakah): Eight Levels of Charitable Giving," Jewish Virtual Library, accessed October 25, 2024, https://www.jewishvirtuallibrary.org/eight-levels-of-charitable-giving.

6. Michaeleen Doucleff, *Hunt, Gather, Parent: What Ancient Cultures Can Teach Us About the Lost Art of Raising Happy, Helpful Little Humans* (Avid Reader Press, 2022), 53.

7. "Stress Resets: How to Soothe Your Body and Mind in Minutes," Dr. Jenny Taitz, accessed October 25, 2024, https://drjennytaitz.com/books/stress-resets/.

8. Jennifer L. Taitz, *Stress Resets: How to Soothe Your Body and Mind in Minutes* (Workman Publishing Company, 2024), 87.

9. David Thomas, *Raising Emotionally Strong Boys: Tools Your Son Can Build On for Life* (Bethany House Publishers, 2022), 69.

10. Thomas, *Raising Emotionally Strong Boys*, 48.

11. Ginny Yurich and Sissy Goff, "Navigating the Anxiety Epidemic," December 27, 2023, in *The 1000 Hours Outside Podcast*, produced by Open Air

Productions, https://podcasts.apple.com/us/podcast/the-1000-hours-outside
-podcast/id1448210728?i=1000639938321.

12. Ginny Yurich and Michaeleen Doucleff, "In Some Cultures They Never
Yell at Children," August 17, 2023, in *The 1000 Hours Outside Podcast*, produced by Open Air Productions, https://podcasts.apple.com/us/podcast/the
-1000-hours-outside-podcast/id1448210728?i=1000624746861.

13. Foster Cline and Jim Fay, *Parenting with Love & Logic* (NavPress,
2020).

14. Foster Cline and Jim Fay, *Teaching with Love & Logic* (Love and
Logic Institute, 2016).

15. Kim John Payne, *The Soul of Discipline: The Simplicity Parenting
Approach to Warm, Firm, and Calm Guidance—from Toddlers to Teens*
(Ballantine Books, 2021), 261.

16. Ginny Yurich and Jennifer Taitz, "Stop Prioritizing Comfort and Dis-
traction at the Expense of Truly Enhancing Your Life," March, 21, 2024, in
*The 1000 Hours Outside Podcast*, produced by Open Air Productions, https://
podcasts.apple.com/us/podcast/the-1000-hours-outside-podcast/id14482107
28?i=1000649989362.

17. Ginny Yurich and Austin Kleon, "Uncertainty Is the Fuel Creativity
Runs On," April 17, 2024, in *The 1000 Hours Outside Podcast*, produced
by Open Air Productions, https://podcasts.apple.com/us/podcast/the-1000
-hours-outside-podcast/id1448210728?i=1000652759483.

18. Ginny Yurich and Jon Acuff, "I Want My Family to Get the Best of
Me, Not the Rest of Me," September 13, 2022, in *The 1000 Hours Outside
Podcast*, produced by Open Air Productions, https://podcasts.apple.com/us
/podcast/the-1000-hours-outside-podcast/id1448210728?i=1000579315329.

19. Kardaras, *Glow Kids*, 127.

20. Jodi Musoff, quoted in Gia Miller, "The Benefits of Boredom," Child
Mind Institute, October 30, 2023, https://childmind.org/article/the-benefits
-of-boredom/.

21. Susan Linn, *Consuming Kids: The Hostile Takeover of Childhood*
(New Press, 2004), 62.

22. Ginny Yurich and Susan Linn, "The Loss of Middle Childhood,"
June 1, 2022, in *The 1000 Hours Outside Podcast*, produced by Open Air
Productions, https://podcasts.apple.com/us/podcast/the-1000-hours-outside
-podcast/id1448210728?i=1000564842154.

23. Nurul Fitriana Bahri and Alvian Fajar Setiawan, "Open-Ended Toys
to Stimulate Cognitive Development Children Aged 1–3 Years Old in the
Pandemic Era," *Journal of Industrial Product Design Research and Studies* 1, no. 2 (February 2023): 45–58, https://www.researchgate.net/publica
tion/376054527_Open-Ended_Toys_to_Stimulate_Cognitive_Development
_Children_Aged_1-3_Years_Old_in_the_Pandemic_Era.

## Chapter 4   You Are Providing Multi-Age Experiences

1. John Holt, *Learning All the Time: How Small Children Begin to Read, Write, Count, and Investigate the World, Without Being Taught* (Da Capo Press, 1989), 162.

2. John Taylor Gatto, *Dumbing Us Down: The Hidden Curriculum of Compulsory Schooling* (New Society Publishers, 2017), 23.

3. Ginny Yurich and Peter Gray, "Don't Ever Look at Your Child's Report Card," July 15, 2024, in *The 1000 Hours Outside Podcast*, produced by Open Air Productions, https://podcasts.apple.com/us/podcast/the-1000-hours-out side-podcast/id1448210728?i=1000662273150.

4. John Taylor Gatto, *The Underground History of American Education: An Intimate Investigation into the Prison of Modern Schooling*, vol. 1 (Oxford Scholars Press, 2017), 63.

5. David Elkind, *The Power of Play: Learning What Comes Naturally* (Da Capo Press, 2007), 152.

6. Peter Gray, *The Harm of Coercive Schooling* (Alliance for Self-Directed Education, 2020), 10.

7. Max Planck Society, "Families Are Shrinking: Study Reveals Shocking Decline in Number of Relatives," European Large Families Confederation, February 19, 2024, https://www.elfac.org/families-are-shrinking-study-reveals -shocking-decline-in-number-of-relatives.

8. Max Planck Society, "Families Are Shrinking."

9. Ginny Yurich and Michele Borba, "We Overlook the Simple Stuff That Doesn't Cost a Dime," January 3, 2024, in *The 1000 Hours Outside Podcast*, produced by Open Air Productions, https://podcasts.apple.com/us/podcast /the-1000-hours-outside-podcast/id1448210728?i=1000640431887.

10. Michele Borba, *UnSelfie: Why Empathetic Kids Succeed in Our All-About-Me World* (Touchtone, 2017), 8.

11. See https://rootsofempathy.org/family/.

12. Borba, *UnSelfie*, 6.

13. John Taylor Gatto, "Our Prussian School System," *Cato Policy Report* XV, no. 2 (March/April 1993): 10, https://www.cato.org/sites/cato.org/files /serials/files/policy-report/1993/3/v15n2.pdf.

14. Gatto, "Our Prussian School System," 10.

15. Charlotte Mason, *Home Education* (Living Book Press, 2017), xi.

16. Charlotte Mason, *School Education* (Living Book Press, 2017), 170.

17. Charlotte Mason, *Philosophy of Education* (Living Book Press, 2017), 240.

18. Nicholas Kardaras, *Digital Madness: How Social Media Is Driving Our Mental Health Crisis—and How to Restore Our Sanity* (St. Martin's Press, 2022), 2.

19. John Delony, *Own Your Past, Change Your Future: A Not-So-Complicated Approach to Relationships, Mental Health, and Wellness* (Ramsey Press, 2022), 60.

20. Ginny Yurich and John Delony, "We Are Streaming and Scrolling Ourselves to an Early Grave," December 31, 2023, in *The 1000 Hours Outside Podcast*, produced by Open Air Productions, https://podcasts.apple.com/us/podcast/the-1000-hours-outside-podcast/id1448210728?i=1000640143294.

21. Katy Bowman, *Rethink Your Position: Reshape Your Exercise, Yoga, and Everyday Movement, One Part at a Time* (Propriometrics Press, 2023).

22. Ginny Yurich and Katy Bowman, "How to Recognize Signs of Movement Hunger," August 7, 2023, in *The 1000 Hours Outside Podcast*, produced by Open Air Productions, https://podcasts.apple.com/us/podcast/the-1000-hours-outside-podcast/id1448210728?i=1000623669682.

23. Ginny Yurich and Dan Buettner, "I Guess I Forgot to Die," August 31, 2023, in *The 1000 Hours Outside Podcast*, produced by Open Air Productions, https://podcasts.apple.com/us/podcast/the-1000-hours-outside-podcast/id1448210728?i=1000626308314.

24. Victoria Dunckley, *Reset Your Child's Brain: A Four-Week Plan to End Meltdowns, Raise Grades, and Boost Social Skills by Reversing the Effect of Electronic Screen Time* (New World Library, 2015), 103.

25. Jonathan Haidt, *The Anxious Generation: How the Great Rewiring of Childhood Is Causing an Epidemic of Mental Illness* (Penguin, 2024).

26. Ginny Yurich and Jonathan Haidt, "The Largest Uncontrolled Experiment Humanity Has Ever Performed on Its Own Children," March 26, 2024, in *The 1000 Hours Outside Podcast*, produced by Open Air Productions, https://podcasts.apple.com/us/podcast/the-1000-hours-outside-podcast/id1448210728?i=1000650483645.

27. Yurich and Delony, "We Are Streaming and Scrolling Ourselves."

28. Peter Gray, *Evidence That Self-Directed Education Works* (Alliance for Self-Directed Education, 2020), 64.

29. Steven Pressfield, *The War of Art: Break Through the Blocks and Win Your Inner Creative Battles* (Black Irish Entertainment, 2002), 146.

30. Peter Gray, *How Children Acquire "Academic" Skills Without Formal Instruction* (Alliance for Self-Directed Education, 2020), 41.

31. Gray, *How Children Acquire "Academic" Skills*, 44.

## Chapter 5  You Are Modeling

1. John Holt, *Learning All the Time: How Small Children Begin to Read, Write, Count, and Investigate the World, Without Being Taught* (Da Capo Press, 1989), 131.

2. Holt, *Learning All the Time*, 130.

3. Holt, *Learning All the Time*, 131.

4. Ginny Yurich and Adelaide Olguin, "We Should Adventure Whenever We Can," January 6, 2023, in *The 1000 Hours Outside Podcast*, produced by Open Air Productions, https://podcasts.apple.com/us/podcast/the-1000 -hours-outside-podcast/id1448210728?i=1000592845739.

5. Ginny Yurich and John Muir Laws, "You're Not Stuck with the Brain You're Born With," November 24, 2021, in *The 1000 Hours Outside Podcast*, produced by Open Air Productions, https://podcasts.apple.com/us/podcast /the-1000-hours-outside-podcast/id1448210728?i=1000542944635.

6. Yurich and Olguin, "We Should Adventure Whenever We Can."

7. Michaeleen Doucleff, *Hunt, Gather, Parent: What Ancient Cultures Can Teach Us About the Lost Art of Raising Happy, Helpful Little Humans* (Avid Reader Press, 2022), 84.

8. Doucleff, *Hunt, Gather, Parent*, 84.

9. Rahima Baldwin, quoted in Beth S. Barbeau, "Learning Through Imitation: Parenting Essentials," Indigo Forest, accessed September 16, 2024, https:// www.indigoforest.com/blog/learning-through-imitation-parenting-essentials.

10. Ginny Yurich and Jean Twenge, "The Two Biggest Things Parents Should Think About," April 27, 2023, in *The 1000 Hours Outside Podcast*, produced by Open Air Productions, https://podcasts.apple.com/us/podcast /the-1000-hours-outside-podcast/id1448210728?i=1000610932310.

11. Ginny Yurich, Joelle Hanscom, and Angela Hanscom, "A Childhood on the Screens Is Not Really a Childhood," February 29, 2024, in *The 1000 Hours Outside Podcast*, produced by Open Air Productions, https://podcasts .apple.com/us/podcast/the-1000-hours-outside-podcast/id1448210728?i=1 000647534665.

12. Ginny Yurich and Heidi St. John, "The Internet Is Forever but Your Children Are Only Children for a Little While," April 26, 2024, in *The 1000 Hours Outside Podcast*, produced by Open Air Productions, https://podcasts .apple.com/us/podcast/the-1000-hours-outside-podcast/id1448210728?i=1 000653666141.

13. Victoria Dunckley, *Reset Your Child's Brain: A Four-Week Plan to End Meltdowns, Raise Grades, and Boost Social Skills by Reversing the Effect of Electronic Screen Time* (New World Library, 2015), 68.

14. Michele Borba, *UnSelfie: Why Empathetic Kids Succeed in Our All-About-Me World* (Touchtone, 2017), 147.

15. Ginny Yurich and Aliza Pressman, "You're Not Giving Up Anything When You Choose to Play," January 25, 2024, in *The 1000 Hours Outside Podcast*, produced by Open Air Productions, https://podcasts.apple.com/us /podcast/the-1000-hours-outside-podcast/id1448210728?i=1000642890835.

## Chapter 6 You Are Requiring Self-Reliance

1. Daniel Quinn, "Schooling: The Hidden Agenda," Ishmael.org, August 16, 1997, https://www.ishmael.org/daniel-quinn/essays/schooling-the-hidden-agenda.

2. Ivan Illich, *Deschooling Society* (Marion Boyars Publishers Ltd, 2000), 29.

3. Alfie Kohn, "What Does It Mean to Be Well Educated?," Alfie Kohn, March 2003, https://www.alfiekohn.org/article/mean-well-educated-article/.

4. Rob French, "These Michigan Colleges Shut Down Because of Coronavirus Concerns," Bridge Michigan, March 11, 2020, https://www.bridgemi.com/michigan-health-watch/these-michigan-colleges-shut-down-because-coronavirus-concerns.

5. Samuel Dodge, "Ann Arbor Canoe Livery Closes for Second Time Due to COVID Exposure," MLive, September 7, 2020, https://www.mlive.com/coronavirus/2020/09/ann-arbor-canoe-livery-closes-for-second-time-due-to-covid-exposure.html.

6. Michael Easter, *The Comfort Crisis: Embrace Discomfort to Reclaim Your Wild, Happy, Healthy Self* (Rodale, 2021), 21.

7. John Taylor Gatto, *Dumbing Us Down: The Hidden Curriculum of Compulsory Schooling* (New Society Publishers, 2017), 7.

8. Ginny Yurich and Nathan Lippy, "There Is Magic in the Mistakes," June 3, 2024, in *The 1000 Hours Outside Podcast*, produced by Open Air Productions, https://podcasts.apple.com/us/podcast/the-1000-hours-outside-podcast/id1448210728?i=1000657685837.

9. Ginny Yurich and Austin Kleon, "Uncertainty Is the Fuel Creativity Runs On," April 17, 2024, in *The 1000 Hours Outside Podcast*, produced by Open Air Productions, https://podcasts.apple.com/us/podcast/the-1000-hours-outside-podcast/id1448210728?i=1000652759483.

10. Ginny Yurich and Heather LeFebvre, "Life Can Be a Great Big Treasure Hunt," June 1, 2023, in *The 1000 Hours Outside Podcast*, produced by Open Air Productions, https://podcasts.apple.com/us/podcast/the-1000-hours-outside-podcast/id1448210728?i=1000615278171.

## Chapter 7 You Are Offering Freedom

1. Carla Hannaford, *Smart Moves: Why Learning Is Not All in Your Head* (Great River Books, 2007), 18.

2. "Average Number of Children Per U.S. Family (Historic), Infographic," Population Education, accessed September 17, 2024, https://populationeducation.org/resource/historic-average-number-of-children-per-u-s-family-info graphic/.

3. "Figure 2-8 Household Vehicle Ownership: 1960–2010," Bureau of Transportation Statistics, September 17, 2015, https://www.bts.gov/archive/publications/passenger_travel_2015/chapter2/fig2_8.

4. "Figure 2-8 Household Vehicle Ownership."

5. Ginny Yurich and Mike Lanza, "Who Wants to Go Outside When No One Is There?," November 28, 2020, in *The 1000 Hours Outside Podcast*, produced by Open Air Productions, https://podcasts.apple.com/us/podcast /the-1000-hours-outside-podcast/id1448210728?i=1000639938418.

6. Mike Lanza, *Playborhood: Turn Your Neighborhood into a Place for Play* (Free Play Press, 2012).

7. Ginny Yurich, Joelle Hanscom, and Angela Hanscom, "A Childhood on the Screens Is Not Really a Childhood," February 29, 2024, in *The 1000 Hours Outside Podcast*, produced by Open Air Productions, https://podcasts .apple.com/us/podcast/the-1000-hours-outside-podcast/id1448210728?i=1 000647534665.

8. Ginny Yurich and Angela Hanscom, "Children Today Are Under Relentless Supervision," October 5, 2023, in *The 1000 Hours Outside Podcast*, produced by Open Air Productions, https://podcasts.apple.com/us/podcast /the-1000-hours-outside-podcast/id1448210728?i=1000630357233.

9. Ginny Yurich and Sarah Mackenzie, "The Transformative Power of the Read Aloud," May 13, 2024, in *The 1000 Hours Outside Podcast*, produced by Open Air Productions, https://podcasts.apple.com/us/podcast/the-1000 -hours-outside-podcast/id1448210728?i=1000655393422.

10. Sarah Mackenzie, *The Read-Aloud Family: Making Meaningful and Lasting Connections with Your Kids* (Zondervan, 2018), 116.

11. Ginny Yurich and Dr. Carla Hannaford, "We Must Reinsert Movement into Childhood," January 13, 2022, in *The 1000 Hours Outside Podcast*, produced by Open Air Productions, https://podcasts.apple.com/us/podcast /the-1000-hours-outside-podcast/id1448210728?i=1000547772474.

12. Ginny Yurich and Katy Bowman, "How to Recognize Signs of Movement Hunger," August 7, 2023, in *The 1000 Hours Outside Podcast*, produced by Open Air Productions, https://podcasts.apple.com/us/podcast/the-1000 -hours-outside-podcast/id1448210728?i=1000623669682.

13. Matt Haig, *The Midnight Library* (Penguin, 2023).

14. Alfie Kohn, *Feel-Bad Education: And Other Contrarian Essays on Children and Schooling* (Beacon Press, 2011), 7.

15. Ginny Yurich and Hannah Maruyama, "College Isn't for Everyone: How to Learn and Earn Without a Degree," June 21, 2024, in *The 1000 Hours Outside Podcast*, produced by Open Air Productions, https://podcasts.apple.com/us /podcast/the-1000-hours-outside-podcast/id1448210728?i=1000659811518.

16. Yurich and Maruyama, "College Isn't for Everyone."

17. Megan Cerullo, "More U.S. Companies No Longer Requiring Job Seekers to Have a College Degree," CBS News, December 5, 2023, https:// www.cbsnews.com/news/college-degree-job-requirement/.

18. Ken Coleman, *Find the Work You're Wired to Do* (Ramsey Press, 2024).

19. Ginny Yurich and Ken Coleman, "Preparing Your Kids for the Work They're Wired to Do," May 8, 2024, in *The 1000 Hours Outside Podcast*,

produced by Open Air Productions, https://podcasts.apple.com/us/podcast
/the-1000-hours-outside-podcast/id1448210728?i=1000654981664.

20. Kohn, *Feel-Bad Education*, 5.

## Chapter 8  You Are Slowing Down

1. Kim John Payne, *Simplicity Parenting: Using the Extraordinary Power of Less to Raise Calmer, Happier, and More Secure Kids* (Ballantine Books, 2010), 141.

2. John Holt, *Learning All the Time: How Small Children Begin to Read, Write, Count, and Investigate the World, Without Being Taught* (Da Capo Press, 1989), 100.

3. "2018 Survey on Recess: New Survey from IPEMA and the Voice of Play Finds U.S. Teachers Place High Value on Recess," Voice of Play, March 19, 2018, https://voiceofplay.org/2018-survey-recess/.

4. "2018 Survey on Recess."

5. Ginny Yurich, Joelle Hanscom, and Angela Hanscom, "A Childhood on the Screens Is Not Really a Childhood," February 29, 2024, in *The 1000 Hours Outside Podcast*, produced by Open Air Productions, https://podcasts.apple.com/us/podcast/the-1000-hours-outside-podcast/id1448210728?i=1000647534665.

6. Yurich, Hanscom, and Hanscom, "A Childhood on the Screens."

7. Ginny Yurich and Kim John Payne, "Low-Screen and No-Screen Kids Are Enduringly Popular," February 6, 2024, in *The 1000 Hours Outside Podcast*, produced by Open Air Productions, https://podcasts.apple.com/us/podcast/the-1000-hours-outside-podcast/id1448210728?i=1000644374754.

8. Ginny Yurich and Sean Killingsworth, "Adults Can't Really Imagine How Bad Kids Feel," September 18, 2023, in *The 1000 Hours Outside Podcast*, produced by Open Air Productions, https://podcasts.apple.com/us/podcast/the-1000-hours-outside-podcast/id1448210728?i=1000628237996.

9. Yurich, Hanscom, and Hanscom, "A Childhood on the Screens."

10. Nancy Jo Sales, *American Girls: Social Media and the Secret Lives of Teenagers* (Vintage, 2017), 62.

11. Yurich and Killingsworth, "Adults Can't Really Imagine How Bad Kids Feel."

12. Sales, *American Girls*, 62.

13. "Constructive and Deconstructive Interference," UConn, accessed September 19, 2024, https://www.phys.uconn.edu/~gibson/Notes/Section5_2/Sec5_2.htm.

14. Gary Brecka, "The Frequency of Authenticity," Hustle | Motivate | Elevate, November 7, 2023, 57 sec., https://www.youtube.com/watch?v=BJWjHL4LBHc.

15. Sales, *American Girls*, 122.

16. Yurich and Payne, "Low-Screen and No-Screen Kids."

17. Ryan Collins, *The God of Tech: Modern Technology, Its Divine Origin, and the Next Great Movement of God Through Spirit-Led Innovation* (pub. by author, 2023), 72.

18. Ginny Yurich and Jerry Kaplan, "Motherhood in the Machine Age," February 19, 2024, in *The 1000 Hours Outside Podcast*, produced by Open Air Productions, https://podcasts.apple.com/us/podcast/the-1000-hours-outside -podcast/id1448210728?i=1000645839749.

19. Ginny Yurich and Ben Angel, "Navigating the AI Revolution," May 1, 2024, in *The 1000 Hours Outside Podcast*, produced by Open Air Productions, https://podcasts.apple.com/us/podcast/the-1000-hours-outside-podcast /id1448210728?i=1000654150726.

20. Collins, *The God of Tech*, 88.

21. Collins, *The God of Tech*, 90.

22. Collins, *The God of Tech*, 91.

23. Madeline Levine, *Ready or Not: Preparing Our Kids to Thrive in an Uncertain and Rapidly Changing World* (Harper, 2020), 23.

24. Levine, *Ready or Not*, 10.

25. Jerry Kaplan, *Generative Artificial Intelligence: What Everyone Needs to Know* (Oxford University Press, 2024), 113.

26. Kaplan, *Generative Artificial Intelligence*, 113.

27. Carla Hannaford, *The Dominance Factor: How Knowing Your Dominant Eye, Ear, Brain, Hand & Foot Can Improve Your Learning* (Great River Books, 2011), 126.

28. Kaplan, *Generative Artificial Intelligence*, 120.

29. Ginny Yurich and Kim John Payne, "We Underestimate the Power of Family," August 10, 2022, in *The 1000 Hours Outside Podcast*, produced by Open Air Productions, https://podcasts.apple.com/us/podcast/the-1000 -hours-outside-podcast/id1448210728?i=1000575715229.

30. Sherry Turkle, "Stop Googling. Let's Talk," *New York Times*, September 26, 2015, https://www.nytimes.com/2015/09/27/opinion/sunday/stop -googling-lets-talk.html.

31. Sarah Mackenzie, *The Read-Aloud Family: Making Meaningful and Lasting Connections with Your Kids* (Zondervan, 2018), 108.

32. Yurich, Hanscom, and Hanscom, "A Childhood on the Screens."

## Chapter 9  You Are Safeguarding

1. Dewey Cornell, quoted in Holly Rosenkrantz, "Bullying in Private Schools Versus Public Schools," U.S. News & World Report, December 13, 2021, https://www.usnews.com/education/k12/articles/bullying-in-private -schools-versus-public-schools.

2. Joy Prouty, *Practicing Presence: A Mother's Guide to Savoring Life Through the Photos You're Already Taking* (Baker Books, 2023), 50.

3. Amy Blevins, "Bullying in Public Schools," *Ben and Me*, accessed September 19, 2024, https://www.benandme.com/bullying-in-public-schools/.

4. Dr. Phil CBS, "'You Never Feel More Alone Than When You're Being Bullied,' Dr. Phil Says, Encouraging Parents to Help Their Child," Yahoo!, October 17, 2022, https://www.yahoo.com/entertainment/never-feel-more-alone-being-225657095.html.

5. Stephen Miller, *The Art of Getting It Wrong: Finding Good in the Misadventures of Life* (Zondervan, 2022).

6. "Bullying Statistics by the Numbers," Pacer's National Bullying Prevention Center, November 9, 2023, https://www.pacer.org/bullying/info/stats.asp.

7. "Bullying Statistics by the Numbers."

8. Kim John Payne, *Emotionally Resilient Tweens and Teens: Empowering Your Kids to Navigate Bullying, Teasing, and Social Exclusion* (Shambhala, 2022), 13.

9. Kim John Payne, *The Soul of Discipline: The Simplicity Parenting Approach to Warm, Firm, and Calm Guidance—from Toddlers to Teens* (Ballantine Books, 2021), 3.

10. Alfie Kohn, *No Contest: The Case Against Competition* (Houghton Mifflin Harcourt, 1986), 114.

11. Kohn, *No Contest*, 9.

12. Ginny Yurich and Alastair Humphreys, "Microadventures," March, 18, 2022, in *The 1000 Hours Outside Podcast*, produced by Open Air Productions, https://podcasts.apple.com/us/podcast/the-1000-hours-outside-podcast/id1448210728?i=1000554466135.

13. Alastair Humphreys, *Great Adventurers: The Incredible Expeditions of 20 Explorers* (Big Picture Press, 2019), 8.

14. Laurie Lee, *As I Walked Out One Midsummer Morning* (Penguin Classics, 2014), 70.

15. Alastair Humphreys, *Against the Odds: The Incredible Struggles of 20 Great Adventurers* (Templar, 2024), 8.

16. Carla Hannaford, *The Dominance Factor: How Knowing Your Dominant Eye, Ear, Brain, Hand & Foot Can Improve Your Learning* (Great River Books, 2011), 18.

17. Susan Linn, *Who's Raising the Kids?: Big Tech, Big Business, and the Lives of Children* (New Press, 2023), 2.

18. Ginny Yurich and Nancy Jo Sales, "Childhood Is Gone," April 10, 2024, in *The 1000 Hours Outside Podcast*, produced by Open Air Productions, https://podcasts.apple.com/us/podcast/the-1000-hours-outside-podcast/id1448210728?i=1000652002327.

## Chapter 10  You Are Choosing the Best Teacher for Your Child

1. Israel Wayne, *Answers for Homeschooling: Top 25 Questions Critics Ask* (Master Books, 2018), 21.

**Ginny Yurich** is the founder and CEO of 1000 Hours Outside, a global movement, media company, and lifestyle brand meant to bring back balance between virtual life and real life. She is a thought leader in the world of parenting, digital family wellness, and the benefits of nature-based play for children. She also has an extensive background in entrepreneurship and building global communities centered on a shared set of values and purpose.

With over one million social media followers, Ginny has built the 1000 Hours Outside movement and brand that now spans the globe, with millions of families committing to restore balance with technology and reconnect with one another.

She is the host and producer of the extremely popular *1000 Hours Outside Podcast*, a top-ranked parenting as well as kids and family show with over nine million downloads since late 2021. She is a keynote public speaker, zinnia enthusiast, and published author. Her bestselling book *Until the Streetlights Come On* (Baker Books) was released in November 2023.

Holding a master's degree in education from the University of Michigan, Ginny has been married to Josh for over twenty-one years. They are lifelong Michiganders and love raising their five children in the Great Lakes State.

## Connect with Ginny:

🌐 1000HoursOutside.com

f 1000HoursOutside

📷 1000HoursOutside

▶ 1000HoursOutside

**1000 HOURS OUTSIDE**